PENGUIN BOOKS

Before I Say Goodbye

Before I Say Goodbye

Ruth Picardie

with Matt Seaton and Justine Picardie

PENGUIN BOOKS

PENGUIN BOOKS

Published by the Penguin Group
Penguin Books Ltd, 27 Wrights Lane, London w8 5tz, England
Penguin Putnam Inc., 375 Hudson Street, New York, New York 10014, USA
Penguin Books Australia Ltd, Ringwood, Victoria, Australia
Penguin Books Canada Ltd, 10 Alcorn Avenue, Toronto, Ontario, Canada m4v 3b2
Penguin Books (NZ) Ltd, 182–190 Wairau Road, Auckland 10, New Zealand

Penguin Books Ltd, Registered Offices: Harmondsworth, Middlesex, England

First published 1998
10 9 8 7 6

Set in 9¾ on 12pt Monotype Imprint
Typeset by Rowland Phototypesetting Ltd, Bury St Edmunds, Suffolk
Printed in England by Clays Ltd, St Ives plc

To Lola and Joe

Foreword

Ruth Nadine Picardie was born in Reading on 1 May 1964 – a Mayday baby. Her middle name was after the South African novelist Nadine Gordimer. Ruth's parents were South African émigrés, part of the wave of liberal intelligentsia that left in the ugly aftermath of Sharpeville.

Ruth was brought up and educated in London, Oxford and Cardiff. She went to Cambridge University, where she read Social Anthropology. Her first real job after graduating was at a film trade magazine, then edited by Oscar Moore. She went on to edit it herself, before getting a break at a (shortlived) women's glossy, *Mirabella*. But she retained a passion for movie-going ever after.

Subsequently, she worked as an editor at the *Guardian* and *Independent* newspapers, but she also developed as a freelance writer for a large and diverse range of newspapers and magazines: from *City Limits* to *Vogue*, and from *Sky* to the *Sunday Telegraph* magazine.

Ruth and I had known each other and had been going out together since our second year at university. We finally married in August 1994. Just after we married, Ruth went for a test on a lump that we had found in her left breast. The results, we were told, showed that the lump was benign. We more or less forgot about it and, later that year, Ruth was offered IVF. The treatment was successful and, in August 1995, our twins Joe and Lola were born.

Just over a year later Ruth went back for further tests because the lump had started to grow. In October 1996 she was diagnosed as having breast cancer. Despite treatment, the cancer advanced aggressively: it was only a matter of months before it became clear that the disease was terminal.

Ruth was going to die, and it became a question only of whether she had a year or two, or just a few months remaining to her.

It was at this point that her elder sister Justine, who had by then become editor of the *Observer* magazine *Life*, suggested that Ruth write a column about her condition. Although Ruth had already contemplated writing about her cancer, she did not feel immediately confident about it. But after writing a couple 'on spec', Justine was convinced that Ruth could do it. The title Justine gave that column was 'Before I Say Goodbye'.

As it turned out, Ruth had time to write only five complete columns before her illness overtook her. When we came to see if we could publish some of Ruth's writing, it was obvious that this material alone was not extensive enough to make a book. So we looked at Ruth's correspondence.

In her last year, Ruth found it increasingly difficult and wearying to keep up with friends and well-wishers: it was impossible for her to see as many people socially as she had once done, or even to answer all the calls and return her messages. E-mail became a way in which she could keep contact with a select group of friends, without any feeling of harassment. Practically, e-mail was also an effective means of maintaining immediate close contact with friends who might be far away: one of Ruth's key correspondents was an old friend who lives in Vietnam. But beyond the practicalities, e-mail for Ruth represented a new and subtly different medium of communication: it was a way of expressing thoughts and feelings more spontaneously than in a letter, yet more reflectively than in a telephone conversation. It had a quality of being simultaneously intimate and serious, yet transient and disposable, and this meshed with something in her writer's psyche.

Ruth knew she had left a rich resource of writing in her e-mail correspondence – in fact, it was her idea that any book of hers might include a selection from them. In compiling this book, I know that we have been carrying out her wishes.

There are hundreds of people – friends, colleagues and readers – who deserve thanks here. I hope they will know that it is only because of exigencies of space and time, and not for reasons of carelessness or ingratitude, that they are not named here. I must thank those doctors, nurses and staff at Guy's Hospital, Trinity Hospice and elsewhere who treated Ruth and did their best for her in increasingly dire circumstances, especially Venetia Herzmark, David Miles, Trudi Coyne, Elizabeth MacDonald, Greig Ramsey, Donal Martin, Jennifer Todd, Liz Watkins and Isabel Bremner. General thanks are due to Antonia Byatt, Helen Birch, Margaret Bluman, Lola Bubbosh, Sam Collyns, Jenny Dee, Alex Finer, Genevieve Fox, Lizzie Francke, Georgia Garrett, Roger Gillett, David and Polly Gilmour, Linda Grant, Nick Hornby, Virginia Hornby, Hilly Janes, Leanne Klein, India Knight, Angela Lambert, Annie Lennox, Andrew Marr, Kate Mosse, Julie Myerson, Peggy Seeger, Charlie Smith, Annette Stevens, Frances Swaine, Jocelyn Targett, Carrie Turk, Beth Wagstaff and Steve Xerri. I owe a special debt to Jamie, India and Carrie, for their generous permission to reprint their personal correspondence with Ruth.

I would like to thank the numerous readers of the *Observer*, *Daily Telegraph* and *Daily Express* newspapers who wrote to me, or who made donations to Trinity Hospice, because of what they read. But especially I would like to thank all those readers of the *Observer* who wrote to Ruth in the first place. They were many, marvellous, kind and moving – in that sense the selection published here is almost arbitrary.

For Hilary Britten, Neill MacColl, Michael Picardie, Caroline and Geoffrey Seaton, I cannot think how best to say thanks other than that this is as much your book as it is Ruth's, mine and Justine's. And lastly, I would like to thank my sister-in-law, Justine Picardie, who was as constant, close and loyal a friend to Ruth as a sister can be, and without whom Ruth's columns might never have been written and this book never published.

Matt Seaton, February 1998

Dearest C,

The latest news is that I didn't have the second lot of
chemo yesterday, because my white blood cell count is still
crap - they went in 'all guns blazing' (direct quote from
oncologist) first time round and it was obviously OTT. So I
have a week off, which is brilliant - like an exam being
cancelled. Next time they will lower the dose from maximum
(7) to almost maximum (6). Meanwhile, my hair is falling out
with amazing rapidity - I estimate total baldness will be
achieved by the weekend, so the whole thing will have
happened in a week. It's getting awfully expensive - had my
hair cut ultra short on Monday, and reckon I will have to
have it shaved on Friday. I was a bit freaked out at first -
it's really alarming running your hand through your hair and
handfuls coming out. Makes you look sick, feel that you are
dying, etc, which I am not - it's simply a function of high
dose chemotherapy. Anyway, I am now used to hoovering the
bed every morning and it's easier to cope with very short
hair. Meanwhile, I am asking everyone I know to buy me a
hat. I hope I don't frighten the children - I imagine I'll
look pretty weird. Just as long as my fucking eyelashes etc
stay in place.

Anyway, at my non-chemotherapy session yesterday I learned
three things.

1) my tumours are hormone receptive (quite unusual in younger
women) which means Tamoxifen is an option if the chemo doesn't
work, though it means I will go into the menopause 2) my primary
tumour may have shrunk by a centimetre or so, though there is a

huge margin of error using a tape measure (sophisticated or what) 3) I fancy one of the oncologists - pure transference, like falling in love with your therapist, since he is not at all attractive though very funny and looks a bit like Dr Green in ER. So that's mildly exciting.

Can't remember exactly what I said to you in my last fax, but the antibiotics started working within 24 hours and I now feel fine. But I definitely overdid it last month. I now realise it's hard to do anything when you're having chemo, given that you have a week of feeling really shitty and then your white blood cell count collapses and you get ill.

I can't believe Far East bureaucracy - have you sorted out a birth plan, yet? I, too, plan to spend the rest of the year having non-hair related beauty / complementary therapy treatments, going shopping, reading novels, etc. Can't believe Fred's bilingual verbal dexterity: Joe and Lola will be grunting for the rest of their lives, at this rate.

All love R xxxx

E-mail to Carrie, 2 December 1996
Dearest, dearest Carrie,
Chemo was vile. I don't fancy Mr Miles any more, since he flirts with all the sad old ladies and I am obviously one of many. Imagine four days of the worst hangover combined with the worst flu, where you can hardly move, feel poisoned, and are half-asleep but not pleasantly out of it all the time. Felt too wretched even to listen to the radio, and didn't want any cheering up from hovering mother and husband. Managed to get up in the morning with the kids for a bit, ditto post-nursery, and that was it. Self Pity Inc. I was only sick once (different anti-emetics), had a smaller dose, but it felt worse (cumulative effect). Uugh. Thank god you can't remember pain (otherwise you wouldn't be having another baby). Four more to go (at least) and I don't even know if it's working. Not sure why some people respond to it

and others don't. Must ask if there's a relationship between devastated white blood cells and devastated cancer cells.

Meanwhile, the Ghost press sale begins on Thursday. Do you want some fripperies sent by Fed Ex? E-mail me immediately.

All love, R xxx

E-mail to Carrie, 17 December 1996
Dearest Carrie,
Thank you for the divine stockings and JOE and LOLA stamps which they will love and, no doubt, decorate the walls with. Lola is currently an obsessive doodler and cutting a molar. Poor Joe on antibiotics again, for ear infection and terrible cough. Both permanently ill (must buy vitamin drops) and talking gibberish.

Matt has perked up, after seeing the breast unit therapeutic nurse. (He'll be seeing her fortnightly from now on.) Also he had a day off the work / childcare grind on Saturday, going cycling in the morning, and to Porchester Baths with Garry and his brother Mark, David and Charlie, to compare willy sizes in the afternoon. But he is being amazingly unsupportive and egocentric – he left for work this morning without saying good luck (chemo this pm). I guess he doesn't have anything left over at the moment. Mum thinks he's in denial, which he probably is, too.

I have been to see a complementary medicine guru recommended by a journalist friend of Justine's who recovered from skin cancer and has been extremely helpful. He is suggesting a whole programme of treatment, ranging from vitamins to low level oxygen administration. In general, what he said made sense ie not 'I'm going to give you shiatsu to make you feel better' but 'You've got a 50:50 chance of survival; Guy's don't know why some people survive and others don't; we're going to make sure you are one of the 50 per cent who do.' The downside is he is a money grabbing wanker, who is charging 2,500 pounds for the first six months' treatment. Matt thinks it's a waste of money and would rather we went on holiday to South Africa and redecorated the house. Ho hum.

Dad is over and all is well because (a) Anne is here to jolly him along and (b) they are not staying with us. The other exciting news is I went to Justine's Chinese doctor (not a poncy Hale Clinic type place but funny old men mixing herbs in Camden High Street) to get Joe's eczema looked at, and who should be seeing Dr Lily before me but Princess Diana. She is stunningly beautiful in the flesh. Went to see Evita the movie, starring Madonna. Quite stirring, once you stopped being embarrassed by the fact that it's a musical. Eva Peron died of breast cancer and guess what: the c-word isn't mentioned once. The great unmentionable.

All love R xxx

E-mail to Jamie, 3 February 1997
Dear Jamie,

Apologies for snail mail paced response: I get so little e-mail that I forget to check it. How are you? I have chucked in the chemo after four cycles (supposed to have six) because it's not having much (if any) effect and I've been reacting really badly to it eg puked during last session, despite intravenous anti-emetics. I have now become allergic to Guy's – last time I went in to see the oncologist I felt really ill for the rest of the day, even though I didn't have any treatment. Am supposed to be starting radiotherapy in the next week or two (every day for six weeks) and I'm hoping I get to have it at St Thomas's. Hey, bet you don't get fun e-mails like this every day.

Fun things about breast cancer:

1. You get your hair cut really short because it's falling out, and it really suits you. You decide to keep it that way forever.

4

2. You can be really horrible to people and not feel guilty.

   Blah blah blah. How's work? Garden? Etc.
   Love love love Ruth xxx

E-mail from Jamie, 7 February 1997
Darling Ruth,
The chemo is a big decision. But I suppose it would have had
an effect after 4 months? It seems to work well for some but
not others. Luck(!) of the draw I suppose. My mate in NYC
who has AIDS and developed bone marrow cancer has had a
miracle recovery and thinks it may be his chemo. He had to
take a week off each month to have his because it made him
feel so shitty. But he knows someone else younger and fitter
who did the same treatment who's just kopped it.
   I started drugs in November after a low T-cell count (for
me, nothing serious compared to lots of others, it was over
200). On the one hand I don't hold much store by such narrow
definitions and anyone's T-cell count can vary by hundreds
depending on whether they've got a cold or whatever. But for
a year I'd been feeling out of sorts which my doctors kept
putting down to HIV. They would. If I went in to casualty
having been run down by a truck they'd say it was
HIV-related. Anyway after only three weeks on basic
treatment (AZT and DdI) they did a test to see how much
virus was in my body (a viral load) and were surprised to
discover I had less virus than their tests can detect. A
good sign.
   I've now upped the ante. I asked to go on a protease
inhibitor (saquinavir) along with old AZT and a drug called
3TC. From everything I can read on the internet etc this is
a good combination. Luckily no side effects as yet. The AZT
depletes white blood cells supposedly and does make you a
little more susceptible to colds (he sniffs, having one
right now). But after lots of research I'm sticking with it.
The recommended doses are much less than people used to be

on hence fewer side effects. AZT is one of the few drugs
that gets through the 'blood-brain' barrier (so they tell
me) and can help reduce any chances of dementia. Rather late
in the day some might say . . .

My T-cell count has gone up by 100 in four months.

If after a year of drugs treatment my viral load is still
undetectable and if I can boost my T-cell count up further
then I may come off them.

If nothing else it makes me feel I'm in control. There's
always the chance that I might be poisoning myself but I
couldn't just let the little bastard virus sit and multiply.
My attitude is if I'm going to go down I'm going to take a
few of the little HIV buggers with me.

Wouldn't it be great if they discovered that all either of
us needs is sunshine, holidays, good food, getting away from
it all and S.L.E.E.P. I sometimes feel that if I went to a
Greek island and spent four months just sleeping, sunbathing
and swimming I'd cure anything. Fuck it, even if it don't
work I'd feel better.

BY THE WAY, X doesn't know about my situation . . . (only
about a dozen people do).

Lots and lots of love. Write sooner and I will too.

Jamie

E-mail to Jamie, 10 February 1997
Dearest Jamie,
Thanks for your brilliant, long e-mail (I also, cheekily,
read the short one to Matt). It feels good to have a friend
who is sick too. God knows, I wish you weren't, but there's
a level of connection that even the most supportive friends
can't achieve. And I do not want to talk about it with the
sad, bald fucks you meet in hospital the whole time.

Re: treatment: there seems to be very little consensus
among my docs. Every one you talk to says something
slightly, but significantly, different about treatment. But
have established that the chemotherapy would have had an

effect by now if it was going to work - they take a more proactive approach at the Marsden, and routinely review treatment after four cycles, whereas Guy's seem to let you suffer for the full whack, regardless of efficacy, unless you take control. Am supposed to be starting radiotherapy tomorrow (every day for six weeks, no washing, no deodorant, eek) but I have a pain in my breast bone which I fear could be secondary bone cancer, so am going to see the docs tomorrow to review situation. (Only because my sister forced an appointment out of them.) If it has spread, I'd 'like' to try another chemotherapy regime, using taxanes (yew tree extract - 'natural' but very toxic, causing total body alopecia!). Oh gawd . . .

You queers are amazing at dealing with HIV. Do you go to counselling or what? Like you say, the fact that you have done so much research and are making treatment decisions must make you feel good. Have yet to get a web browser and find breast cancer site. Part of me is so exhausted by all the appointments and X-rays and tears that I want to switch off from the subject completely. Re: alternative stuff. The number of treatments / therapists is (a) overwhelming and (b) expensive but I'm dabbling a bit. Can't be any less effective than the fucking chemotherapy, and doesn't make me feel shitty. But if second chemo and radiotherapy fail, then I will be on every mad diet and consulting every bearded healer in the business.

Glad that your drug combo is going well, with no side effects. (Crass aside: do you watch ER? Jeannie has HIV and is feeling sick cos of drugs.) Re: blood brain barrier. I think I'd rather go nuts than die in agony. Or maybe you can do both.

Doing a bit of work - in fact off to interview Joanna Briscoe (novelist) this pm. Keep in touch.

Luurve Ruth xxx

Dear Ruth,

I'm really glad you think it's of any help at all sharing
thoughts. I'm just so shocked and surprised to find a healthy
big ride of a bird like you in, if not the same boat, then
any boat marked by the hand of Cain. Less likely than you
for some reason ... but then people say the same to me.
I've grown so used to not talking about the 'condition' or
diagnosis that it comes as a relief to me to be able to chat
away about it.

I wouldn't say I'm glad HIV happened, but it sometimes
feels like a terrifying mind-expanding drug that I would
have been less of a person for not having experienced. Just
wish like other such drugs I could now give it up.

At least Life becomes a case of collecting your thoughts
not your pension. Not necessarily a bad thing ...
philosophically.

Alternative stuff: I do sometimes try visualisation. Not
organised hand-holding stuff. Just throwing the monster out
of individual organs and parts of the body ... like
Sigourney Weaver finally chucking out the alien in said film.
Oh whilst we're at it ... I really would try anything. Just
between you, Matt and entre nous and all that ... I started
a course of anabolic steroids in November. Lots of evidence
in States that building muscle mass can help delay onset of
wasting conditions. Read the article ... bought the needles
and the gear ... Getting bigger by the day. Hey, you breast
cancer girls need to find an alternative treatment that makes
you feel horny and look gorgeous too. Well, all body
alopecia sounds quite sexy actually. No pube bumps.

The other thing that must be more difficult for you is the
family etc. The main reason I keep my stuff strictly limited
publicity wise is I couldn't face dealing with sorrow,
grief, whinging, sympathy, worry and shit. Other people's
reactions in other words. What a fucking nightmare. Not an
option in your case, but I really don't envy the hassle.

Lurv ... Jamie

E-mail to Carrie, 12 February 1997
Dear Carrie,
Hope is beginning to fade this end since it looks like I
have secondary bone cancer. Haven't had all the tests yet
(X-rays yesterday, bone scan on Friday) but I have pain in
my sternum which suggests the monster has spread. So
radiotherapy has been delayed a week while they find out
what's going on. The treatment for bone cancer is also
radiotherapy, but they need to extend the field. They will
also hit me with Tamoxifen, sooner rather than later.

I obviously have bionic breast cancer - I want the primary
tumour to be hung, drawn and quartered after my death. So
it's good you're coming over in April - at this rate, I
won't be around much longer. Justine continues to be
amazingly supportive and helpful - thanks to her, I am now
seeing the same doctor every time (sexy Dr Miles, who is
also the least patronising and most open). The Marsden
pretty much said what Guy's said, so I won't be transferring
there.

Ho hum pig's bum. Hope to be more cheerful some time soon.
Love love love R xxxx

E-mail to India Knight, 13 February 1997
Dear India,
Test results on Tuesday, but I know in my bones (fnar fnar)
that something is up. So sweet of you to offer money - by
selling children? - but I'm as happy as I can be with my
treatment so far. Also for your offer to help - at the
moment I'm trying to live as normal a life as possible, but
I shall expect you to supply me with crack when the Nurofen
stop working.

You are only a very small elephant. How's the mad diet
going?

Love R xx

E-mail from Jamie, 13 February 1997
Ruth,

What the fuck is your cancer up to? So typical of you . . .
never doing anything by half measures. You don't have some
normal little cancer; you have a Terminator machine.

When I was first diagnosed the prognosis was five years
maximum. I lived with the threat which was continually
repeated by ass-hole doctors that my health could go from
fair to D-Day in as little as a couple of months and I used
to shock myself into insomnia with stories about people
whose immune systems collapsed almost overnight. Ten years
later I'm lucky to be alive at all. To be honest it was more
fear than goals that kept me going. Not fear so much of
AIDS, but the fear that since I couldn't put my parents
through dying of THAT I'd have to kop myself. In those days
suicide was so much more respectable than the big A.
Scareylands.

Last year I definitely felt the wind had changed . . . the
disease was entering a new and something's definitely 'up'
phase. Like that terrible moment when you know you've food
poisoning but you're not ill yet . . . Just a taste in the
mouth . . . premonition stuff. I've been putting a positive
(ho ho) gloss on the stuff. But when my T-cell count reached
210 it was only 10 (ie insignificant) from the official AIDS
diagnosis as opposed to just HIV positive. I've minor
complaints which my doctors say are HIV related . . . sinus
problems, odd bouts of diarrhoea. No big blobs on my face a
la Tom Hanks.

Doesn't help me imagine what you must be feeling right
now. As different as the experience of seeing a storm on the
horizon (and just getting wet), and running for cover here's
the bitch of a hurricane. I know in my heart of hearts after
so many funerals and friends dying that I'll probably die
quite soon (maybe another five years if I'm really lucky) but
I've still got the energy to make myself believe that I
won't. I'd spit on anyone who said to me 'hey, maybe you
should just deal with the imminence of your own death'.

Wouldn't you just want them to be run under a bus that afternoon? But I suppose I've shaped my whole life the last few years around some sort of termination. No mortgages, no financial commitments, until recently no boyfriend (who do you tell, when, how . . . so much better to keep it casual).

I wish there was some way they could give you five years. 5 years is such a long, long time. Who needs eternity . . . when you're running out of time 5 years is a whole eternity on its own.

Listen sorry I got into a depressed mode but my god if you can't get depressed about death what the hell can you?

Lots of love, and PS I've steered clear of all the heavy emotional stuff like kids and motherhood, Matt and family, because I didn't want to put you on the spot. If you want think of me as the guy in the cell next to you.

PPS. Life After is the next big thang. Surprising how this changes all our cynical reductionism.

E-mail from Carrie, 15 February 1997
Dearest R.,
What news from the latest round of tests? We are losing sleep at this end over your bone scan, as you no doubt are at that end. Have re-read your email 500 times and decided that when you wrote, you did not KNOW that you had bone trouble, you were just suspecting on the basis of sternum pain. Please God, let this be the case and let the tests have confirmed nothing more than muscle strain from picking up 2 heavy twins at a time.

Have another minor reason why you cannot die. You are 99% of the glamour in my life: you are the only person I know who hobnobs with royalty in quack waiting rooms, you wear lipstick better than anyone I know and your legs are the longest of any woman outside the glossies. You could still carry off a miniskirt whilst all I can wear is tracksuit pants. Very sexy.

Hope your husband remembered Valentine's day. Mine didn't.

Just in case Matt forgot, which I'm sure he wouldn't, I love you anyway.

 XXCXX

E-mail to Jamie, 16 February 1997
Darling Jamie,
Until now, breast cancer hadn't been at all painful (unlike the fucking treatment) apart from the occasional bit of tenderness round tumours. But, since simple Nurofen (not even Nurofen Plus!) is doing the trick, we're not talking major pain - just a background throb. Actually, it's receded a bit this weekend, so maybe the whole thing was a false alarm. Oops. Shoulda switched on the disassociation button. Results tomorrow.

 Can't tell you why / if the C is on the march, and neither can the pea-brained oncologists. A bearded, yoga-practising Kathy Acker type would say that it's marching on because the chemo compromises your immune system, but it's pretty compromised anyway, otherwise I wouldn't have cancer.

 God I know what you mean by fear of getting brain sickness. (Breast cancer spreads typically to the bones, liver, lungs and - less common - brain.) On Thursday I couldn't remember the word opportunistic and went into a complete panic.

 I don't know how you have survived without telling the whole world and his aunt about your status - don't you want sympathy, empathy, chocs? I know there's shit involved, too eg endless fucking phone calls demanding detailed analysis of your emotional and physiological state. Sometimes I feel like putting a message on the answerphone. 'Hi. Ruth thinks she has secondary bone cancer. Luckily, she is feeling less weepy today (Sunday). Thank you for calling.'

 Shall we make a silly film to show on BBC2 after our deaths? Over-exposed and black and white to make us look gorgeous, lots of slo mo running on the beach and Tom Cruise and Nicole Kidman narrating our e-mail correspondence.

 Bye!! R xxxxx

Dearest Ruth,

I know - Wendy told J yesterday and I was going to send you
big weepy message last night and then thought better of it -
it's hardly as if you needed depressing further. On the
other hand, cyberchitchat seems inappropriate. If you have a
minute, please explain - any chances AT ALL of radiotherapy
etc making this go away? What happens now? How is Matt
coping?? Oh poor Matt, I can't bear it - poor everyone.

Write or phone if you can. MAKE me do something to help,
even if it's just chocolate parcels. And please let me know
how it's going, if you can.

Lots and LOTS of love (and from Oscar) India xxx

Shall I have a mass said for you? It worked a bit last
time I did it (for my granny).

India XXX

E-mail to India, 19 February 1997
Dearest India,

I like cybercancer better than phone-cancer - makes me less
prone to weeping, boredom, self-pity, etc. The statistics
are that I have an 18 per cent chance of surviving more than
five years. I imagine the chances of surviving for more than
10 years are very small. Essentially, advanced breast cancer
is terminal.

Obviously this is a total headfuck, but I think the HIV /
AIDS approach is a good one ie accept that I have a terminal
illness, that I am not going to live for three score years
and ten, and then be positive about maximising length and
quality of time I have left. That means keeping healthy,
embracing orthodox and complementary treatment, and having a
good time. Cancer is all about fear, secrecy and euphemism -
palliative care, advanced disease - all are euphemisms for
dying. Oncology is the biggest euphemism in the world. But
there is another way.

You can help by NOT sending me chocolate - I am already

11 stone and Tamoxifen (oral hormone therapy - like being on the Pill) can make you put on weight. The cancer diet (a la Liz Tilberis) hasn't kicked in yet. Do light a candle for me - it's nice to be remembered. Matt is being stoical, though God knows how much fear and misery he is repressing. You can help him by keeping in touch, asking how he is - I seem to be getting all the attention at the moment. This applies especially after I am dead. You can arrange the flowers at my funeral, too. (I love sweet peas, so hopefully it will be a summer one.) Can you handle all this honesty?

Love love love Ruth xxx

E-mail from India, 19 February 1997
Dearest Ruth,
Well, I'm so glad you aren't taking a Mavis Riley-style 'I think I'll just die now, please' approach (I would). You're so right about people with Aids / HIV - constant source of amazement to me, and so are you.

Eleven stone - why, you're practically a waif. Come and stand next to me and you'll look like you're in profile. My diet is sort of on hold - it appears I can either be fat and happy and shopping at Evans or normal-sized and really bloody grumpy and hateful. What to do?

What cancer diet? Raw stuff?

Do you think there would be any point in you seeing a healer? My mother knows a v good one called Matthew Manning. I don't suppose he works miracles, but one can't help feeling that as there's nothing to lose you MIGHT AS WELL . . .

Keep cybercancer reports coming. Lots of love (and to Matt).

PS Say if you want to meet (we could bring our laptops and sit next to each other, tapping away, to minimize weepy behaviour / embarrassment at not knowing what to say).

xxxx India

E-mail to Jamie, 19 February 1997

Dearest Jamie,

Let's cut to the chase, here. Cut the crap. Face the music.
And trot out every other cliche in the book: I have
secondary bone cancer ie stage 4 breast cancer ie advanced
breast cancer ie an 18 per cent chance of surviving for more
than five years. The reason I would like to swap diseases
with you is this: cancer is all about fear and euphemism
(see stage 4, advanced, also 'palliative care'). Why don't
they just spell it out: you're dying, sucker! And what the
fuck is an 'oncologist'? They can't even say the C-word.
Instead of being frightened about those percentages (and the
chances of living 10 years are probably not even worth
talking about), why not embrace the fact that I am gonna die
young and beautiful (I wish) and then be positive about the
time I have left, both in terms of maximising health and
having a good time. This is the HIV / AIDS paradigm, no?
It's called politics.

How is your hooting going? I thought the Kathy Acker piece
was a stream of consciousness mess which couldn't win anyone
over to her cause - no evidence, just her declaration that
'I'm cured' - nine months after diagnosis, with no objective
assessment? Yeah, right, Kathy, see you in the hospice in
five years' time. On the other hand, you've got to survive
mentally and if this is how she does it, then good on her.
After all, she'd probably die after tons of horrid orthodox
treatment, too. (Like me.) The weirdest thing is the double
mastectomy on grounds of 'symmetry'. Right, I'd like both my
legs cut off, too. Talk about A Zed And Two Noughts. I
reckon mastectomy is an extension of her interest in body
fetishism: tattoo yesterday, pierced labia today, mutilation
tomorrow. I expect Orlan is planning something similar.

You deserve a hero boyfriend: how could anyone survive
terminal illness - no, that's cancer talk, how about HIV -
without one? I think Cameron is a cool name. He sounds
perfect. Can he cook? Relate to hedgehogs? Obsess
over ER?

I definitely want our correspondence to be published posthumously. (Lots of money for our widowers.) How about The Diary of Ruth and Jamie. 'In 1997, two young people [I'm going to be 29 in my obits] went into hiding in South London when their bodies were occupied by invading Bad Cells. This is their moving diary . . . Blah blah blah.'

I'm completely with you about expecting the worst, then you can only be pleasantly surprised. So felt very neutral when I made Dr Death phone me up with results. He had his patronising, 'Now, Ruth' voice on. Though have had a few weeps since, since I am now accepting the inevitability of death.

Keep chanting. Resist the temptation to come over all American and blurt out 'I love you' to all your friends.

Yours,

Anne Frank

E-mail to Carrie, 20 February 1997
Dearest Carrie,

PLEASE keep the so-called trivia coming: the last thing I want to do is spend 23 (instead of 22) hours a day thinking about cancer. I want life to carry on as normal as much as possible.

I started radiotherapy and Tamoxifen on Tuesday and no real side-effects so far apart from a little tenderness in my breast. It's been a very tough 10 days since I noticed the pain in my sternum, then waiting for the test results. But I feel I have made a lot of progress, emotionally, partly through long e-mails from a friend who is HIV positive (though largely in the closet about his status). Whereas cancer is steeped in fear and euphemism, HIV and AIDS is about recognising the prognosis (ie an early death almost certain) and then being positive (geddit) and maximising the quality and quantity of the time that remains, through the best treatment, a positive attitude, good times, etc.

One way of coping is denial ie certainty that you are

going to be one of the few that make it. I feel I can cope best by accepting that I have an 18 per cent chance of lasting five years ie despite all the euphemistic crap about stage four, advanced breast cancer, management, palliative care, that I am going to die sooner rather than later - could be this year, could be five years, might even be 10. That way, the fear and dread of new symptoms disappears. (Eg I have upper back pain which probably means it has spread there, too. Now I accept the reality of the situation, it's not such a disaster.)

I felt the same about infertility - that hoping and praying for a baby was disempowering and that by saying, 'We can't have kids' I took control and could let go of some of the grief. And of course a miracle happened in that case - we probably had an 18 per cent chance of producing Lola and Joe, so maybe our luck will hold.

I know this isn't your approach at all, but I hope you can understand why I feel this way right now. Which isn't to say that I have given up or that I want to die. I intend to have the best palliative care (horrible horrible phrase) which is very good these days, keep trying the cranky stuff, eat well, get fit, have a nice time and be around for Lola and Joe as long as I possibly can.

On that sombre note, I'm off to the hospital. More trivia soon.

Love you lots. R xxx

E-mail to India, 23 February 1997
Dearest India,
Radiotherapy isn't nearly as bad as chemo (thus far) - so far just tired and have slightly sunburned skin (though this will get worse over the weeks). Never saw the Matthew Manning programme, but am writing to someone recommended by a friend - loony but I'm happy to clutch at straws.

X left a message last week and I had no idea who she was. I'm afraid I have no intention of going to the science

museum with her, rude as that sounds, since I am sick of
being everybody's favourite cripple - you wouldn't believe
the number of acquaintances who suddenly want to be your
best friend and feel they are entitled to regular, blow by
blow accounts of your emotional / physiological state. 'But
Ruth, how ARE you?' they ask, meaningfully. Rubber neckers.

Oh dear I seem to have got rather angry.

Had dinner last night with American couple who live in the
nicest loft I have ever seen, in Kentish Town of all places.
Suffering from severe property envy. But the rent is 350
pounds a WEEK, so I can dream on.

Love love love Fatty xxxx

E-mail from Jamie, 25 February 1997
Dear Dear Dear Ruth,
Thought I'd start on a light note. Funerals.

I have a very silly but unconquerable belief that I'll be
floating in some sort of state watching things after my final
demise. It's just such a groovy idea and so convincing that
I can't seem to shake it. But I'd like to go straight there
from the Departure lounge, and not pass go or waste time
with a funeral.

What's really annoying is the idea you get a set amount of
time for the funeral. Forget that. If people insist on
having one for me I want it to be like one of these
Wagnerian epics. Days on end. The Bayreuth of Burials.
Special effects, ballet dancers, hampers with food,
orange-sellers, and ice cream breaks. How can you pick one
pathetic shitty little poem I never really liked but someone
thought I did, and a couple of lines from Shakespeare, some
naff speech, halting lines from some semi-religious text and
me in the coffin shouting 'get a fucking move on and play the
records for fuck sake'.

Maybe the trick is to make the funeral go on for far too
long. Say three days with hotel accommodation rolled in. By
the end of it people hate you so much they're glad to see

the back of you. 'Self-important cow! Who the fuck did she think she was?'

Half-seriously. If I started to fade why couldn't I have my funeral before I died? I'd love to be there and hear the tributes and be able to thank them all in person. Then I'd go away to die and promise to disconnect my mobile.

Isn't it so utterly bamboozling to discover that something so beautiful, fantastically talented and unique as me or you depends on some clump of dysfunctional plasma-balls or calcium concentrates. Cells, bones, bits of old seaweed waving in the blood. So irritating. Like talking to a very stupid bank clerk.

You didn't sound your normal chipper self. I diagnose a severe case of fresh air. Noticed you were out with J and L in parks and stuff. Big mistake. All that nature. Elements, trees, soil . . . decay. It's all Carmina Burana mortality. Bound to make you morbid dear.

Next time I promise to talk about other things.

Lots and Lotsa Love

Jamie

E-mail to India, 25 February 1997

Dearest India,

Why have you never been featured in Homes & Gardens? Or perhaps you have. Don't you love the way journalists lie: 'dusty' pink? How about screaming fuchsia? And, 'She intends to redecorate with a more subtle bone-coloured scheme.' Oh yeah? So how come she's lived with unsubtle pink for three years.

Radiotherapy breaks up the day completely, since most of my appointments are at 11am / 11.30am. On a good day (ie no waiting around), whole thing takes an hour, including travel - on a bad day (i.e. hospital running late) two hours. I sometimes sleep in the afternoon, but that may be because I sleep so badly at night and nothing to do with the radiotherapy at all.

Have you tried Philosophy Products? (Available from Space NK.) Fab. Can't you write your anti-health column for Jeremy's new supplement?

I did an insane thing yesterday. Matt and I are going away for our FIRST NIGHT WITHOUT THE KIDS in a couple of weeks' time - Gravetye Manor in West Sussex, where we spent our wedding night. I'm writing about it for the Observer, so it's a freebie. So instead I just blew 425 pounds on underwear (including stomach hiding silk slip) from Agent Provocateur. Stupid, or what? But I look like such a slob most of the time, and Matt will be so excited and, what the fuck, I'm dying. You can wear it after I've kopped it.

Bye!

From A Pig.

PS Bought a Fuse yesterday. Very disappointed - too much wafer. Prefer my sweets chocolatey. Have you tried the new limited edition mint Kit Kat? Yum yum.

E-mail from India, 25 February 1997
Dearest Ruth,

My God, I'm writhing with jealousy in my mammoth grey bra and huge granny knickers. FOUR HUNDRED AND TWENTY-FIVE QUID! Bloody hell. But what bliss. Please describe IN DETAIL items of underwear (yuck, I sound like a perv). It's such a lovely shop, isn't it? Being a sad housewife, I rather covet the furniture AP stock as well. My only AP possession is a pair of red maribou-trim satin mules with vertiginous heels - very sexy, although of course since we have two children we tend not to MATE, and effect is rather spoilt by cellu-legs and attractive stubble. And the sad fact that I can't walk in even the dwarfest heels.

I would love to have your underwear after you've copped it, but I fear you seriously underestimate my stupendous girth. Perhaps I could wear your knickers as remembrance bracelets around my outsize wrists.

Love & kisses Fatface xxx

Dearest R,

Sorry for silence. Only excuse is shrieking toothache which
has culminated, 20 mins ago, in the extraction of a rotting
wisdom tooth. Local anaesthetic still in operation,
so am seizing the opportunity to write before the pain
kicks in.

Re: early death. I don't like to think of the diminished
survival chances. But I've decided that if you are
heroically confronting the likelihood of an early death,
then your friends must also. You can't be left alone
pondering your shortened lifespan and it will not help if
people around you act like they don't know what you really
have to face up to. So I'm not clutching on to the miracle
cure theory. That said, I do harbour a number of fantasies
(1. you live long enough for effective, symptomless
treatment to be found 2. they got it wrong, again, and
you've had somebody else's scan / test results all along
(let's face it, so much has been wrong there must be a
chance of this one) 3. this is all a horrible nightmare
which will dissipate in the morning). But I know these are
fantasies and are only there for momentary comfort. They
make things worse, actually, when you stop fantasising and
come back to reality. I favour more optimistic targets, eg,
let's say secondary school for the kiddies. But I understand
why you must take things in small steps. It is a good and
more manageable strategy to set yourself achievable targets
to give you a sense of progress.

Will write again when the toothpain recedes.

Much love, love, love xxCxx

Dearest Ruth,

Quite good, cancer of the forehead. You could get out of
every single commission by claiming cancer of the thumb,
bottom cancer (can't sit down to type), cancer-induced

allergy to paper ... At least your cancer is respectable. Think of the poor people who, as if having cancer wasn't bad enough, have things like cancer of the anus, where sympathy upon being told is tempered by sudden desire to BARK with laughter. Or maybe I'm just a horrible, unfeasibly shallow person.

Not much to communicate apart from that a strange Finn keeps e-mailing me.

Lots of love xxx Porky (I hope you don't mind my insensitive C.O.T. anus joke)

E-mail to Jamie, 4 March 1997
Fellow prisoner Jamie,
25 minutes until the kids arrive home from nursery, so here is rapid e-mail from your bad, neglectful friend on DD-Cup. There's been a lock-down here and no mail going in and out for a week, but am hoping this will get out.

This pm went to 'self-help' group (yuk - pass the lemon sponge, will you dear) for women with secondary breast cancer which meets once a month at Tommy's. Was dreading whole thing - imagine bunch of sad old ladies drinking tea. Instead a bunch of sad young(ish) ladies drinking tea. And eating chocolate biscuits (good quality - so much better than prison food). Still reckon I was the youngest there. (Brownie points for me.) Only five prisoners in total, plus two warders, including GHASTLY breast care nurse at Tommy's, in huge floral kaftan and slacks, Nana Miscouri (sp?) glasses. Fashion victim, moi? Quick to judge, moi? Just like Alison Steadman in Abigail's Party. And her manner - so humourless. Anyway, liked the other women, one of whom had reached Zen-like state of acceptance. Partly awful visions of the future, too - one woman, age 50, diagnosed seven years ago, talked about pain relief and hospices, which I am totally not yet ready for, existentially. Anyway, should be interesting. And worth 18 months' extra time.

Have you outed yourself yet? How's work going? What was
the outcome of your viral load?

I'm a tiger. I'm a tiger. (Self-help chant.) Aagh. Seven
minutes until kids get home and haven't made supper. Will
write again soon.

Big kisses. Roar xxxx

E-mail from India, 11 March 1997
Dearest Ruth,
The problem with you being ill is that when I don't hear
from you I fret and worry, almost certainly completely
needlessly. This must be very annoying for you, knowing that
people are thinking, 'ooh, I wonder if she's ok' when you
are probably just busy or can't be arsed to e-mail. So I'll
assume you're okay and moan about myself instead.

I don't think I can go to Style party because I am so
obese. Seriously. I don't know WHAT has happened in the past
2 days - period is due, which doesn't help - but I have
BALLOONED to inhuman proportions. AND I have nothing to
wear. And, worst of all, I got so sick of having so many
(about 50) white hairs that I foolishly just dyed it, and as
any moron knows you should NEVER use black hair dye unless
you want to look like a Goth, but I was desperate and broke,
so couldn't go to N. Clarke (besides I wouldn't fit into the
seats and it would be embarrassing). And so now I look like
a fat, currant-eyed, many-chinned, OLD, TRAGIC Goth. FUCK.
And on holiday I had nice skin and now look like I have
facial boils, as well as facial cellulite (of the cheeks).
Do admit the deep gloominess. And I've just had a row with
Jeremy, whose work crises are turning him into what Alan
Clark might call a complete spastic.

Also, I hate my house, which is minuscule & thus always
messy and grubby, and I hate my garden, which is simply a
huge cat toilet. Also Archie fell into a flower pot and got a
fat lip, and I feel so sad for him every time I look at his
poor swollen little face.

Do other people being grumpy make you irate? I mean, at least I haven't got cancer. Oh moan moan moan.

With love, & fatly, I

E-mail to India, 13 March 1997
Dearest India,
Yes yes I'm here and in the cyber dog house, e-mail wise.
The last couple of days have been ridiculously busy. On
Tuesday had radiotherapy, then lunch with my sister, then
acupuncture with Dr Big Yin Deficiency Lily, then evening out
in beloved Stokie, just round the corner from you - not
particularly nice pub on the corner of Church Street called
the Rose & Crown - to celebrate our friend Charlie's 40th
birthday. Nearly called in, but was after 11pm. Then
yesterday, cycled to Bayswater to interview dull Australian
feminist, then cycled to Guy's for treatment, then cycled to
Dickins & Jones for 'personal beauty consultation' at the
fabulous, fabulous personal beauty studio. (Waiting list:
One year - it's the only place in London (I think) which is
independent of the beauty companies.) I have turned into a
gay man, I think, since I spent 269 pounds on products
(consultation is free). But the man is a magician (name:
John Gustafson, American, camp though married with two kids)
and lovely. I wanted a minimal routine which made me look
brilliant but not as if I was wearing make-up, and I am now
truly in love with Prescriptives moisturiser and virtual
skin. I am a Fashion Bimbo. In evening went to Twins Club
Committee meeting - now there's thrilling - and felt even
more superior than usual. I know I'm a puritan, at heart, so
I am busy finding my inner Shallow Fashion Bimbo before I
die.

I'll try and come to the Style party after the kids are in
bed, but I may have to collapse. Matt will be there, in any
case. I don't believe you are too fat and ugly to attend -
you ALWAYS look fabulously well-groomed, chic, elegant,
stylish and make me feel even more like an overgrown

student. Get your name down on the waiting list at D&J - at
least you're never too fat for cosmetics.

Have been sleeping badly since the children were born -
nine months of them both waking up, and now being ill - I
think I do all my unconscious worrying at night. I tend to
sleep very lightly, have horrible night sweats and wake up
early. Having said that, the last couple of nights have been
better so maybe the Chinese herbs are doing the trick.

Please carry on moaning - I hate it when people can only
talk about cancer. I know exactly what you mean about house
being too small - however big one's house, you always expand
to over fill it. But your house always looks fabulously chic
and clean. Ours is truly disgusting - perhaps we should get
a cleaner. So fucking dusty all the time. How big a house
would you like? I am fantasising about three bedrooms and
two studies ie five bedrooms. Peckham here we come.

Shame about weather going horrible. I cycled through
St James's Park and Hyde Park yesterday, and practically
swooned over crocuses, daffodils and cherry blossom.

Am obsessed with Pret a Manger. Think about it all the
time. Perhaps we should go for lunch there some time?

Love love love R xxx

E-mail to India, 17 March 1997
Fellow face cream addict,
Why does J. Gustafson live in Walthamstow? Surely he is paid
a fortune? He was certainly wearing several hundred pounds
worth of see-through shirt when I saw him. And why married
when he is so very camp? I've been on the waiting list since
August, so no leapfrogging. Am going back in a couple of
weeks to have my eyebrows shaped (queen of the fashion
bimbos). Didn't say anything about going back to States. In
fact, studio seems to be expanding, if anything. You will
never look like a mother in a gravy ad, even if you go and
work for Bovril.

Smoked salmon de luxe is mine. What is your fave Pret AM

sandwich? Also like passion cake and real lemonade. How are
the exciting pre-school activities going? Took babes to
London Transport Museum on Friday, by bus. They loved the
bus bit but I don't think the museum is brilliant for
toddlers (though Joe liked pretending to drive a bus). Both
are cutting canines and generally miserable. Joe woke at 5am
this morning and wouldn't go back to sleep.

How was your weekend? My head hurts - am sure I have
cancer of the skull.

Love love love R xxx

E-mail to India, 19 March 1997
Darling India,
Hooray, hooray another epic from you. I get so sick of: (a)
writing health oriented e-mails to friend who is HIV
positive (b) writing heavily emotional e-mails to friend who
is in Vietnam.

So hooray for shallow, cake-oriented moaning.

My life as a fashion bimbo continues: yesterday bought
pair of linen trousers (elasticated waist) and linen shirt
from Hobbs (my new favourite shop, though size 16 jacket was
too tight) and new pair of (brown, three strap)
Birkenstocks. What is happening to me? But it is such good
therapy. I wish summer would hurry up: I never know what
shoes to wear in the winter. Immediately afterwards had
long, boozy and hugely delicious lunch with Angela Lambert
(used to work with her on Independent), lovely, thespy old
bird who did everything in the Sixties - single parenthood,
illegitimate daughter. Bertorelli's in Covent Garden is my
new favourite restaurant in the whole world - just as nice
as fashion victim Oxo style places. Anyway, she had just
interviewed Matthew Manning, rates him and has got me an
audience with him: another 50 quid down the drain (perhaps I
should buy a pair of trousers, instead).

Who are you interviewing Robbie Williams for? V. exciting.

I, too, have cancer of the eye socket. Also cancer of the

heart (racing heart) and cancer of the lungs (breathless).
Seriously paranoid about every ache and pain, but I have
genuinely bad feeling about skull pain (which has spread to
eyebrow / eye socket). Looked at my bone scan again which
looked 'hot' in the right place. Not that a fucking doctor
would notice.

Have booked holiday to Majorca: 91 pounds return,
including tax, infants free. Probably some clapped out
Albanian charter plane that will take 48 hours. Going 12 to
26 April. Can't wait.

R xxx

E-mail from India, 20 March 1997
Dearest Ruth,
Oh, the bliss of your e-mails.

Interviewed Robbie (to his friends) for Style; became
slightly in love. He turned out to have shrunk – hurrah! –
and was pretty LISSOM & foxy. He gave me big juicy stories
to write about – drugs in Take That, and how he used to nick
the others' groupies out of spite, which made me laugh a
lot. (I once went to bed with someone called Sam Markham
purely to spite a foul girl called Lucy Watson, who once
said 'I'm threatened by your body' – how puky can you get??
Not much more, I don't think.)

In fact I've had an excellent day – catpoo-killing machine
came, found a brilliant and exceptionally speedy cleaner &
then chatted to Robbie and then ate 2 banoffi pies in a cafe
in Notting Hill. So nice when you KNOW you've done a really
good interview – it's only happened once before, with Chris
Eubank. V attractive youth, I must say – he is a charming
mixture of arrogance, chronic insecurity, deep sexiness and
v good jokes. Quite flirty, but then am deluded no doubt &
probably reminded him of his mother (although enormously
made up, for impact).

Are you sure skull / socket troubles aren't sinuses?
91 quid absurdly, suspiciously cheap – how fun though. I

want to go away in time for 5th wedding anniversary in May. Am very pleased about the retail therapy & spectacular casting off of perhaps slightly puritan ethic. Jealous of Birkenstocks - I SQUEEZE my feet into ordinary shoes and hobble around in agony. So wish I was the kind of girl who could wear Manolos, which sadly is impossible because feet are perfectly square. Only wear Adidas at the moment which, despite scrupulous foot hygiene, remain desperately stinky.

ER is coming so I'll go. Can't wait to go to sleep to dream of Robbie.

LOTS of love xxx India

E-mail to Carrie, 23 March 1997

Dear C,

Have I told you about my new life as a bimbo? Suddenly into body maintenance - make-up, clothes. Yesterday had a pedicure. Ludicrous but more effective than therapy.

Will write again soon. Love love love R xxx

E-mail to India, 3 April 1997

Dear Rock Chick,

Am really fed up since, after WEEKS of faffing (from Guy's) and hassling (from me) they have confirmed that I was right all along and have bone 'involvement' (great euphemisms for cancer of our time) in my skull after all. I also have - totally unrelated - an 'infarct' in my right hemisphere ie dead tissue that you get after a stroke, and very unusual in young people. So I probably have some weird neurological disorder as well as breast cancer. All this means that next week is going to be non-stop visits to the hospital, to sort out radiotherapy to skull, new treatment to strengthen bones, etc. And I am going to barricade myself in to the hospital until they give me a total body scan, to establish exactly just how far the cancer has spread. I am very breathless at the moment and worried about my lungs. But

they are scandalously laissez-faire - would rather wait
until you're dying until they do anything, rather than treat
you pro-actively. This has characterised their approach from
the word go. What I want to know is are they lazy?
incompetent? or trying to save money? Seriously considering
changing hospitals. Meanwhile, have to fit in endless,
tedious complementary appointments, plus going to Suffolk at
the crack of dawn on Monday to be 'healed' (ha ha) by
Matthew Manning.

Matt has been illegally reading your e-mails to me. I found
him chuckling over the computer last night, saying they were
'hilarious'. Please feel free to be rude about him.

Jeremy will stop moaning after his groovy bachelor hol in
NY. All men hate domesticity, don't you think?

Face looking v. old and crepey, despite designer face
cream.

Lola still exploding from both ends, poor bunny. Cruel, v.
tired mother sent her to nursery, anyway.

Love from misery fat gut xxx

E-mail to Carrie, 5 April 1997
Dearest C,
Well, after weeks of hassling (by me) and faffing (by Guy's)
it turns out I do have skull 'involvement' (lovely
euphemism). Plus they have discovered an infarct (dead
tissue, like after you've had a stroke) in my brain, which
the bone specialist tells me is completely unrelated to my
cancer, so either (a) he doesn't know what he's talking
about or (b) I have some incredibly rare neurological
condition, too. Perhaps it is better to end one's life as a
vegetable, rather than in pain. Anyway, more fucking
treatment looms, though not before I gun down the entire
oncology department in an effort to get an MRI body scan, so
we can establish what exactly is going wrong, where.

Went to a healing circle yesterday - embarrassingly sad
and desperate thing to do. V. worried about men with beards,

clammy hands and baggy trousers, as in cult, but lots of
blue-rinsed old ladies and regular types. Supposed to go on
a 'mental journey' while holding hands and listening to new
age bonging, but all I could think about was abdominal
bloating. Going for one-to-one session on Monday (have to be
in Suffolk at 9am - mum is driving me). At least easier than
eating shark cartilage every day.

Kids' illness nightmare now over, though they both have
bad coughs and Joe is cutting canines and is in agony. Also,
I think I have flu. What a week.

Must go and feed kids baked potato. Write soon.

Love R x

E-mail to Carrie, 10 April 1997
Dearest Carrie,
Thanks for your long, loving e-mail and sorry for my
silence. My whole life seems to have been taken over by
illness. This week, for example:

Monday: trip to Suffolk to see healer, Matthew Manning.
Tuesday: appointment with Michael Baum (head of cancer
treatment at UCH); secondary breast cancer group meeting at
Guy's; appointment with Guy's. Wednesday: appointment with
complementary practitioner (biomagnetic therapy). Thursday:
day off. Friday: acupuncture.

After holiday, have decided to confine complementary
appointments to one week a month, so life will be less
dominated by illness. Having said that, will have to have a
course of radiotherapy to my skull, which is becoming
increasingly painful - spread from forehead to eyesocket and
cranium. So I guess my left eyelashes, eyebrow and left lot
of hair will fall out, which will be very attractive, not to
mention the burn marks on my forehead.

You're absolutely right that, if they'd taken me seriously
when I first reported the pain in my head, I could have had

it all blitzed in one go. They haven't been sitting on any
results, it just took weeks to convince them I needed a CT
scan because X-rays aren't sensitive enough. I think from
now on they won't fob me off. So, for example, am booked in
for CT scan of my chest to check out my lungs, since I am
breathless at the moment (hopefully this is just a
post-radiotherapy effect). But, according to the oncologist
I like and respect, aggressive, pro-active treatment
of secondary breast cancer does not lengthen life,
compared with the British / NHS passive, symptomatic
approach.

This is very counter-intuitive to accept, and I think
American oncologists would disagree, but the former approach
can certainly interfere with the quality of life: loads of
tests and loads of treatment. I wish they'd told me this
before. I feel like I'm fighting the NHS the whole time - but
at least stroppy cows live longer. I've insisted that the
neuro-radiologist looks at the brain infarct, which they
will re-scan in three months to see if it's growing.

The latest spread is bad news only in the sense that it is
evidence of the disease's inexorable spread, as yet
unchecked by Tamoxifen / acupuncture / etc and it means more
bloody treatment. But we knew I had secondary bone cancer,
anyway, so it's not a huge disaster. The really bad news
will be if / when it spreads to the liver. I was only joking
about turning into a vegetable, but I am starting to want to
know exactly how one dies of breast cancer. How did your
father die? I hope it's not some lingering lung collapse,
but brain secondaries which put me in a coma. I still can't
quite believe I'm going to die and, deep down, assume that
there will be some miracle. You're right about pain relief,
though I still have a lingering dislike of medication - my
body is a temple and all that. But let's face it, the temple
has been completely desecrated already.

Don't worry about meeting the Elephant Woman on 1 May
(really hope you can come: have booked a room at a
restaurant in St John Street, EC1, called The Peasant, for

8.30pm). My hair is short but not thin any more. And am not all tired and drawn because the best therapy I have discovered is spending a fortune on designer face cream.

Love you, R xxxx

Dearest India,
Thanks for Robbie piece which, sadly, am unable to read because I can't work out how to download a text file. So your mad last para remains unread - aren't endings a bugger? I always peter out oddly.

Are you starving to death yet? We didn't get our organic veg delivered this week (holiday planning) so are living off vile fridge remnants eg spaghetti with sausage and tomato sauce and stir fried cabbage (I kid you not).

Shopping latest: have spent 122 pounds on Lazartigue hair products. Think I have gone mad. If my luggage gets lost en route to Gatwick I will have lost a million pounds in toiletries.

Miss you. Ruth xxx

E-mail from India, 24 April 1997
Dearest Ruth,
Hurrah! Are you back? I have missed our correspondence greatly, hence nerdily eager 1st-day-back missive. Did you have a nice time? Are you brown? Did the babies like sand?

I have nothing much to communicate. Am dying to vote (& to celebrate your birthday) but I haven't got a voting card yet, v worrying as I do so long to return Diane Abbott. The only thing that's happened since you left is that I have BALLOONED further, existing on diet of tarte au citron (testing) for a week because have no funds to buy proper food.

Oscar started school and is loving it, thank God. His teacher is like Miss Honey in Matilda.

Boy George has been in papers as he is being sued by one
Kirk Brandon, of band called Spear of Destiny, for
suggesting the two were having sex many moons ago. Very
oddly, Susannah phoned in state of high excitement & said,
Well, you'd know all about sex with Kirk. And it turns out
that APPARENTLY, according to her elephantine memory, me
and Kirk once did it. What is really peculiar is that I have
ABSOLUTELY no recollection of this whatsoever. She swears
it's true & says she was in the room at the early snogging
stage. Isn't it odd of me to forget, though? Surely I'd
remember a little bit? I'm sure she's got it wrong. Now am
very worried about who else I may have inadvertently snogged
- Michael Winner? Robin Cook?

Not snogged Robbie, though. Very tragic story. Beginning to
suspect he LED ME UP GARDEN PATH in exchange for kind story.
How cruel. Or perhaps he was ashamed of idea of 2 fat people
merrily bouncing along together, eating pies and not fitting in
seats. Because I must say I am so fat I even shock myself. Look
like I'm made out of partly-baked (ie beige) dough.

Do write back as soon as you can. Things have been v bleak
on the cyber front - keep getting junk e-mail & no
entertaining letters. Everyone is so boring.

What birthday present would you like (paid tomorrow)?

LOTS of love I'm glad you're back & love to M&J&L too xxx
India

E-mail to India, 8 May 1997
Dearest India,
Hold the front page. On Tuesday we found out that the
'disease' (euph TV) has spread to my liver and lungs. Have
been told I only have a few months to live. Beginning new
course of chemotherapy tomorrow, which may give me a few
more months. Definitely time to find a new godmother.

I cannot BELIEVE that Jeremy voted Tory. You must divorce
him unless he recants.

Love Ruth xx

Darling Jamie,

Do you really have to take one of your drugs with grapefruit? Sounds dangerously complementary to me. Mind you, Guy's are pumping me full of yew tree needles.

Have you bought your flat yet? It's great being a cripple. I am waiting for my disabled car sticker (so chic), free cleaner, and 50 quid a week disability living (aka dying) allowance.

Ruth: The Movie would be great. Maybe you should make it after I've pegged it, otherwise people won't be able to fake the emotion. Then you can show it at my funeral, Oscar Moore style. We've borrowed a Hi-8 Sony video camera from friends who live in Vietnam and buy state of the art electronic goods in Singapore, so the kids will know what I looked like (tired and self-conscious).

Had a terrible afternoon, yesterday, in Paperchase, weeping whilst trying to buy 'memory boxes' for the kids, to fill with letters, photos, etc. Slept all afternoon but amazingly didn't wake up with puffy eyes.

ER tonight, which gives life meaning.

Love love love R xxxxx

Dearest Ruth,

Are you actually IN the hospital? Or at home? Oh arse.

I can't send you weepy why-oh-why missives every day, so I am going to carry on as normal, and if I bore the pants off you in the process pls write and tell me. I suppose now you can safely carry out the 'I never liked you and you smell of wee' school of 'pal'-shedding.

Have been reading papers about Fat Robbie Williams, who is apparently off to the drying-out bin. And looking at the photos, in which he appears to be made out of dough, I really wonder how I possibly entertained the idea of tongue-less snogs in Top London Hotels. (Happily Jeremy has

stopped being insane, and we are off on a love trip to
Morocco at the end of the month - 1st time w/o the kids in
5 years.)

I'm not going to keep on asking gruesome questions, but
are you going to have to end your days in a hospital bed, or
can you stay at home? Do you believe in God? (It's ok, not
going to start sending you neo-Christian Cheerful Thoughts
Of The Day, although would be quite a good joke to do so
solemnly, no? Or coming round to your house with guitar &
sing Kumbayah while staring at you weepily.)

Fiendish Oscar is home from school and I must feed him.

LOTS of love India xxx

E-mail to India, 10 June 1997
Dearest India,
A million apologies for my silence. I have become (even more
of) a bitter, angry, envious, depressed old cow who can't be
bothered even to read her e-mails. Think I must start taking
anti-depressants. Anyway, please keep sending me your
e-mails, the only good ones I get (apart from Jamie's).
Everyone else says: 'Had a marvellous weekend in Devon!'

I am not in hospital at all, except on chemotherapy days
(once every three weeks). I feel pretty well, other than
tired and downhearted, and both Matthew Manning (who I saw
yesterday) and my Chinese doctor both say I am much better.
But I have a huge tumour in my liver which I can feel. They
are going to scan me after the next chemotherapy session,
when we'll find out what's really going on. If it's working,
I'll carry on with the chemotherapy and might have a year's
remission; if not it'll be curtains this year which I really
can't believe since I am not in pain/losing weight/etc
etc. Hence no blowing of savings on round the world trip
since I think I'm in denial.

Sadly, I am a Top London Atheist but death-bed conversion
to Judaism not yet ruled out. Should be able to go over to
the Other Side at home, while attractively attached to

drips, oxygen, etc, with children posing sadly but beautifully one on each side of bed, while I (at last) have fashionably lost three stone. Trying to plan funeral but worse than wedding in terms of deciding where / how to do it. At the moment thinking of burying ashes in scenic churchyard near Steyning so children have place to visit.

John Gustafson is the nicest man in the world - he sent me a load of beauty freebies. But why does he live in a flat in Walthamstow? Very odd. Perhaps he spends all his money on clothes, in manner of working classes.

A Fashion Victim Writes retired due to illness, but am coming back as A Cancer Victim Moans. That will be interesting.

Never thanked you properly for birthday bath goodies - sadly, sexy oils have not improved sex life though vanilla lip salve is new best friend.

Hate my hair: bushy, dull brown and impossible to grow out.

Have you read Diary Of Bridget Jones? Brilliant.

Love from a fat whining moo cow xxx

E-mail from India, 13 June 1997

Dearest Ruth,

We went to look at massive house in lovely Vicky Park last night & have decided we are definitely NOT moving. It's the Stokie Summer Festival this Sunday - do you want to come? Lots of kids' entertainers, bouncy castles in park etc and lots of dogs on strings and lesbians too, hurrah.

Lunch on Wed would be lovely. Huge bummer, I must say, to have cancer & be fat. But perhaps you're only pretending - when I saw you you looked v slimline. Where shall we go? Can you drink, or does it interfere with treatment? Quite feel like getting pissed in sunshine. Shall I book somewhere, & what neck of woods do you want to be in? Maybe Momo? Let me know asap bcs it gets all booked up.

I've agreed to go on a week-long 'fasting walk' for Style.

You walk 15 miles a day and exist on fruit juice, water & herbal tea. Not only this, but IT'S IN GERMANY. The horror. No doubt I'll collapse, become delirious and start singing Tomorrow Belongs to Me while frantically biting into German people's calves, mistakenly thinking they are made of wurst.

I've found the most brilliant summer dress at M&S, Ghost-style with a frill.

Lots of love India xxx

Observer Life, *22 June 1997*

You're 32, a stone-and-a-half overweight, depressed by the stains on the sofa and have never come to terms with having piggy eyes but, still, life is pretty great: you've got a husband who can make squid ink pasta and has all his own hair, your one-year-old twins are sleeping through the night and, as for your career – well, you might be interviewing George Clooney next week.

And that lump in your left breast, the one you noticed after you stopped breastfeeding last summer? In the squid ink / Clooney-filled scheme of things, the hospital would smile and tell you not to worry, it was the harmless fibroadenoma they'd found in 1994. But this is the fat, stained, piggy-eyed parallel world of illness, and your lump, I'm sorry to say, is actually cancer. Or should we say lumps, because, oops, it's spread to the lymph nodes under your arm and in your neck, which means it's stage three cancer and you've a 50:50 chance of living five years.

As you'd expect, the diagnosis turns you into a grumpy, bitter, envious old cow. After a fourth acquaintance tells you their aunt has breast cancer, you realise you don't feel sorry for any post-menopausal woman who has the disease because fiftysomething isn't a bad crack at life, especially if your kids have grown up. You start feeling resentful about the amount of money that goes into HIV research and complaining about having a non-glamorous illness. (Aids = pretty men who die young. Breast cancer = old ladies in wigs.) You ram a non-organic carrot up the arse of the next person who advises you to start drinking homoeopathic frogs' urine. Appeals for the seahorse conservation project go straight in the bin.

The strange thing is that, alongside all this anger, the Clooney-luvin' Pollyanna inside you just won't give in. OK, so the cancer has spread to the lymph system but, because surgery is now futile, at least you don't have to have a mastectomy and then die anyway, breastless, five years down the line. All right, the chemotherapy means you have to hoover your hair off the pillow every morning, but it's finally forced you to have your bush cropped, which would look fabulously Jean Seberg if you weighed less than 10 stone. And, hey, it's not food combining, but perhaps the chemotherapy will help you lose weight.

Then, in February, when the disease spreads to your bones, your oncologist tells you that this is the 'best' secondary breast cancer to have, because the skeleton isn't a vital organ and you can live with it for years. Also, there's nothing like terminal illness for not getting divorced. As for not seeing your babies grow up, better to have had half a life with your beautiful children than a whole life without.

Finally, in May, seven months after the original diagnosis and five days after your 33rd birthday, you learn the disease has spread to your liver and lungs. Abruptly, you enter the bleakly euphemistic world of palliative care. Pollyanna commits suicide. Your chic crop turns into a toilet brush. You're so grumpy and depressed you start believing your children would be better off without you, sooner rather than later. You even go off *ER*.

Still, it ain't over till the fat lady's thin. Or until her liver packs in. Or something. Watch this wig.

Dear Ruth,

I woke up this morning, knackered as usual, too late a night
last night, made worse by 7 year old son coming into our bedroom
at 2.00 am following a nightmare. It was pouring with rain, my
period had arrived and I was preparing myself for a glum old
Sunday. I then picked up the Life section of the Observer and,
attracted by the picture of two beautiful children, the happy
smiling couple and the tragic story of cancer, I started
reading. My shock and horror at learning it was YOU who had the
cancer and that it was REALLY serious and not a joke struck me
dumb (and put rain, sleeplessness, period etc all sharply into
perspective). I have read your witty, warm and intelligent
articles for ages. I have actively sought out 'Ruth
Picardie' from the morass of newsprint that arrives every
Sunday on our doormat. I grew to love you and feel you were
the sister I never had when I read about your struggles with
babies, broken nights, childcare and work schedules. You
always made the working mother seem a real person, not a
Superwoman, but always competent. I am horrified you have
such a horrible illness. You are far too young and far too
nice for this to happen to you. There's nothing I can do to
help, but you and your family will be in my thoughts often
and I wish you well in whatever of life is left. (I shall
also be praying for a miracle.)

   With my love,
   Jenny Fanshawe

Dear Ruth Picardie,

I read your piece in yesterday's Observer. I've also read
other things you've written, though I cannot now remember
what you wrote about. But yesterday I was in tears. I don't
know what I can say, and I will probably say the wrong
thing. I only know that it seems important to say something
and try to let you know that I wish I could do something,

anything, to help make a little more bearable what is
happening to you. My immediate thought on reading what you
wrote was, what an amazing woman.

I have just ended radiotherapy treatment for cancer, after
a previous hysterectomy. I'm supposed to think that once
I've recovered from this everything will now be OK, but who
knows - life now seems fairly uncertain. I am 52 tomorrow,
and I have two grown up children of 33 and 30. In a way I
thought that well, if I didn't survive, at least the kids
are grown up - but hang on, I haven't got any grandchildren
yet, this means I'll never know them. From your vantage
point of 33 years, 52 probably does seem like a fair crack
at life, and in some ways it is, but the trouble is that
once you reach that age, it seems very unfair not to be able
to have my statutory three score and ten, and hey, what
about all these 104 year olds that we keep reading about.
Also, I wasn't menopausal (at least not very) and now,
wombless and ovaryless, I've been hurtled headlong into it.

What you write seems to capture the utter unreality of
your situation, that there you are with all that going on in
your body but at the same time you are carrying on doing the
usual everyday things, and even writing about it for God's
sake. Where are you getting the energy? What comes through is
the sort of person you are, full of passion, humour, love and
bravery, in spite of, or probably because of, also being able
to admit to being 'grumpy, bitter, envious and depressed' - and
very angry too I should think, about what has happened to you,
and also the disparity in interest and funding between AIDS
research and services, and cancers affecting women.

I hope that you are surrounded by people who love you, and
who can support and hold your hostile and despairing
feelings, and also be with you when a little bit of joy
comes creeping in, against all the odds.

I send my love to you, and to your family, and look
forward to keeping in touch with you through the Observer.
Susan Davis
Brighton

Observer Life, *29 June 1997*

I'd always thought social workers were good sorts underneath, unfairly maligned as bearded, interfering family-destroying, do-gooders. But recently – thanks to the Cleveland backlash backlash – I had begun to think of them as self-sacrificing super-heroes second only to comprehensive teachers.

That was until last week, when I was allocated one of my own. Alerted by the local social services that my 'care needs' were to be assessed by a member of the disability team, I became, well, perhaps not incandescent, but certainly breathless and headachey with rage. How *dare* they! How dare some *stranger* come barging into my house, snooping around and passing judgement – after only the most superficial of acquaintances – on whether I was sick enough to merit a subsidised cleaner. Is this what journalists do all the time? No. I was the victimised subject of a Channel 4 documentary; the heroine of a Ken Loach film who'd had at least three of her children stolen into care.

Then, a few days before my assessment, I began to panic: after all, I *wanted* a subsidised cleaner. My groovy 1960s childhood had made me a wannabe minimalist architect whose children obediently lived in a cupboard. And yet, after a lifetime of liberal horror at the concept of *paying* someone else to clean the toilet, I was now fed up with being too scared to turn on the light in the 'en suite' bathroom in case a stain came out from behind the U-bend and bit me on the bum. My toddlers had turned basic household maintenance into a full-time job (yes, darlings, of course you can do action painting after supper). More importantly, when you're supposed to spend the last months of your life surfing in

Australia, or writing a brilliant novel, or being a fantastic mom, it just seemed too sad to spend every day staring at the cobwebs and struggling to lug the hoover up the stairs.

Monday was a bad – aka slut – day, when I didn't get dressed or leave the house; ate old, cold pasta straight from the fridge; whined to my oncologist about the return of bone pain in my skull; and slept all afternoon. This would have looked great on the subsidised-cleaner assessment form. But on Tuesday – just like the moment you finally see the emergency dentist – I started feeling a lot better. Disaster!

So then I began to plot. I got dressed, but left the breakfast dishes in the sink. I turned off the radio (sad people with terminal cancer surely don't dance around the kitchen to Greater London Radio, certainly not sad people who need subsidised cleaning) and hoped that Snoop would notice the collection of painkillers left casually by the phone.

My social worker, it turned out, was nervous, had trouble with her spelling and possessed amazing two-inch nails. She asked me whether I was still with the children's father; I ostentatiously swallowed my morning dose (12 capsules) of Chinese herbs. She said I didn't look sick; I omitted to mention that my schedule of hospital visits, sleeping, reading and saving myself for the children also included regular lunch dates. I offered her a cup of coffee: she awarded me two hours of subsidised cleaning, twice a week.

So it turns out that social workers aren't so bad, after all. But as for contract cleaners . . . I like to think of myself as the sort of tough, urban chick who screams at executive cleaning agencies for sending staff who omit to wipe the skirting board. Now, I imagine, I'll have to endure some depressed, underpaid, slow-motion work-experience teenager in a Day Glo overall who thinks cleaning is redistributing dirt. I'm breathless and headachey with rage.

Dear I,

Help! I am in serious e-mail debt: four from you, at least, to my zero. So glad you had a nice holiday. Did the children die of loneliness? Did you die of loneliness without them? Does having sex mean you are now pregnant (Ms Fertile)? My libido is DEAD. Most of my pubic hair has fallen out because of the chemotherapy. I look like an alien. Yuk yuk yuk.

Have got my cripple's driving disc and disability living allowance of 50 quid a week. Hurray, double yellow lines here I come. I love social workers.

It is so cold I have the central heating on. In Wimbledon week. Only interested in watching Boris.

Feeling more cheerful. Perhaps because I went to the Bristol Cancer Help Centre for a day last week which was full of chanting, kaftan wearing vegans but reminded me that you can't give up hope because (a) people who believe they are going to die tend to die sooner and (b) living without hope is miserable. Went to Steyning for the weekend and ATE MYSELF STUPID. Matt's mother is a brilliant cook.

Love R xxx

Dearest Ruth,

Did you know that there actually exists a porno mag called Big & Fat? Find this reassuring - if ever careers came to entire standstill & I was forced to eke out a living to support hungry children & starving Jeremy, could just reveal rolls of flabulous stomach to pervos for money.

I am very worried because for 4 days now I have been in the grip of the most APPALLING & constant nausea. Now before we left Crete, we had a very ill-advised meal at a v scuzzy taverna (the kind that says CHIPS HERE). I only had 2 mouthfuls (amazingly for me) & was immediately aware of off-anchovies being present. So most probably I've got some sort of awful food poisoning. However, thought of sprogdom has occurred. Damn & blast. I never know when my period is due either, which doesn't help. Anyway – I'm sure it's just illness because we used sturdy condoms, and they've never failed us before. (The taverna menu also said SAUSAGE & NEGGS, GAKE, ICE-GREAM.)

Oscar off school with awful flu-like cold (me too). He's just said 'I'm going to the loo, as quietly as 61 mice.' He is a most peculiar little being, I must say. Archie just fiendishly naughty: he has just decorated a bar of soap with yoghurt, very carefully, and rubbed it all over the sofa, in space of 20 seconds when I wasn't looking.

Had dinner with my mother last night – she was on v good form & screamingly funny, having discovered that a friend of hers used to manufacture vibrators. You can imagine my mother's disgust – she says she was shouting at the friend saying 'I am freakishly uptight & finicky! I BEG you not to say any more!' But the friend relentlessly went on and on as Mummy went pea-green. Anyway – she asked after you & when I said you weren't brilliant she shouted 'STOP! STOP! If you say anything negative she is going to get worse.' Then she MADE me tell her that you were going to be mended completely, then made me visualise you skipping about, pubic hair intact, in the flowers & sunshine, after which she was happy. So now I have strict instructions that if anyone asks I am to say you are soon to be blooming with rude health. She is bonkers as conkers, of course, but possibly right.

Back on Sunday, will write then.

LOTS of love I xxx

Letter from reader, 21 July 1997
My Dear Ruth,
I felt I had to write to say how much I admire your courage. It isn't easy to disclose to the world and his wife. Since I began nursing back in June 1974 I have met so many brave women who reduced me to tears with their fortitude.
I have seen so many people defy the odds but make no

mistake you have a steep hill in front of you but you can
reach the summit.

   Now before you throw this in the bin I know you said you
are sick of hearing stories of recovery and I can understand
that. I was diagnosed with Hepatitis C in '94 and I know in
the end that only a liver transplant will buy me more time.
There were times when if one more person said maybe they
will find another treatment, I think I might have punched
them in the mouth. I had to retire from health visiting
(remember those busy bodies who undermine your belief in
your mothering skills) and I was pissed off big time.

   I had a year of chemotherapy which reduced my weight by 2
stone and my hair by half. Mind you I looked wonderful in an
anorexic translucent fashion and if I had the energy I could
have taken up several affairs which came my way.

   I found two things really helpful. Brick Throwing: Stand in
the garden scan the horizon for cats, husbands etc. then hurl
the brick as hard as possible. The second thing I did was talk
talk talk and talk. To friends, husbands, kids and strangers.
Never underestimate the kindness of strangers. Do your
homework, do your own research, don't be a passive patient, all
the research shows snotty patients do best. Ruth I wish I could
hold your hand and tell you you can do it.

   Nursing on the wards nearly finished me off as I could not
understand why people had to suffer. I still remember the
first patient of mine who died just before Christmas '74. Her
name was Mary Flowers aged 32 with 2 kids and what sticks
with me is we never allowed her to talk about what was
happening. I feel we denied her the chance to get better
because we denied her feelings and fears.

   It doesn't matter if you bore the arse off everybody you
know because there will always be somebody to listen. But
you will find out who your friends are and you might be
surprised.

   When I became ill people I had given hours of time to
vanished. Still it saved me wasting any more time on them.

   I grew up in an abusive family (the works: physical,

sexual, emotional) and becoming ill gave me the courage to
sever ties with people who had no relevance in my life.
There is probably scope for several pieces in that. On that
score I have always enjoyed your writing over the years. You
sound like a real person with real problems just like the
rest of us. How to fit in the shopping get my legs waxed and
still have energy enough to entertain the frightful bores
that my husband's work depends on. I am sure people think if
you write for Cosmo you must have it sorted, not so I guess.

Whilst I was doing some canvassing in the House of Commons
I met a well known Lord who writes. He was kind enough to
give me tea (and make offers). He said people think if you
are well known you never feel lonely and crave company but
it wasn't true. So often reality is a let down.

There was one other thing I did and that was to set up a
phone help line for those affected by Hep. C. This has been
helpful for me because I realised I wasn't alone and I felt
able to help and contribute something.

God don't I go on but this comes from the heart to wish
you well. And if you ever need an ear to bend feel free.

With love and best wishes
Gabrielle Page
Skenfield

Observer Life, *27 July 1997*

Everybody thinks cancer makes you thin. In fact, I'm getting fatter and fatter. I know this because people keep coming up to me and saying, 'You look so well.' Actually, I don't look particularly well – I'm pale and my hair is falling out behind my ears, as if I'm a failed street gang member whose zigzag shaving has gone wrong – so what they really mean is, 'You look so fat.'

A couple of people have been even less subtle and said, out of the blue, 'Are you on steroids?' If you're a man, this means: 'Gosh, you've got huge muscles.' Unfortunately, if you're not a man, this means: 'Gosh, you've got a huge arse.' To make me look less greedy, I usually lie and say, 'Yes', when, actually, I only take steroids for five days every three weeks, before and after my chemotherapy. Which is a bit like saying my son is 'on' steroids because we sometimes put hydrocortisone cream on his eczema.

Things could be worse: my counsellor still asks, politely, as a measure of health, 'How's your appetite?' when she could just as easily burst out laughing and say, 'Still pogging yourself, then?' Nevertheless, I can now only wear clever Ghost clothes with elasticated waists. And I'm not happy.

Why? For a start, having a terminal illness is supposed to make you extremely wise and evolved, turning you into the kind of person who thinks, 'What is being 11 stone compared with the joy of seeing my children run through a flowery meadow as if in a junior Timotei ad?' Unfortunately, I just can't get my head around Zen meditation, and seem to be stuck in, 'Why did I eat the fishfingers that Lola spat out when I can't fit into my jeans any more?'

More importantly, I'm now halfway through my second

course of chemotherapy and I was hoping for a little pay-back: something – a couple of cheekbones, say – in return for the aching veins, the puking, the headaches, the disastrously thinning eyebrows. It does happen: I got a letter this week from a woman whose treatment made her look 'wonderful in an anorexic translucent fashion and if I had the energy I could have taken up several offers which came my way'. I wish! Instead of toying with a little home-made broth at lunchtime, I have developed an obsession for crisps; and, as for my longed-for George Clooney interview (and subsequent elopement): no show. (I keep trying to blame the crisps, if not the George Clooney non-interview, on steroids, which were originally developed to help concentration camp survivors put on weight. Then I remember I'm only taking them for five days every three weeks.)

Why am I so fat? Before anyone mentions the term 'comfort eating' can I just say that cancer isn't just about getting round to reading *Middlemarch* before it's too late: it's a full-time job keeping up with the eating opportunities. Yes, we cry at the breast cancer support group which meets once a fortnight, but there's always a huge tin of biscuits, including chocolate ones. The best way of killing time at the hospital? I find that eating sandwiches works rather well. And what can friends do to help? Why, a hamper from Fortnum & Mason has been shown to reduce tumours by up to 50 per cent! As for exercise, forget it. Do you think I'm going to brave the communal changing room at the swimming pool with no pubic hair?

Short of getting heavily into morphine (not quite as chic as the heroin that models use to stay thin, but, hey, this is the NHS), my chances of leaving this world in anything smaller than a size 16 urn now depend on adopting one of the so-called anti-cancer diets so popular with bearded American gurus. These include the Breuss Juice fast, the Kelly regime, grape fasting, Dr Moerman's diet, Dr Alec Forbe's Bristol diet and, most Teutonic of all, the Gerson diet, which involves 'eating' only freshly pressed organic fruits and vegetables and having coffee enemas on the hour. Yum! And so convenient, too.

A slightly more humane option is advocated by the Bristol Cancer Help Centre, where I spent a day last week. In order to 'strengthen ourselves physically, emotionally, mentally and spiritually, and to promote healthy immune and repair functions', the centre recommends we avoid red meat, caffeine and 'excess' alcohol, sugar, salt, fats (especially hydrogenated ones) and dairy produce, smoked or pickled foods, preservatives and additives, processed food. What a fab way of losing weight while pretending not to.

My new life on the Bristol anti-cancer non-diet began well, with a lunch of aubergine couscous, carrot and bean stew, and green salad, followed by nut slice. Tea-time, I have to say, was a bit of a disappointment, featuring some very dry oatmeal biscuits and decaffeinated tea. But I rallied on the train home with a 'grab pack' of cheese and onion crisps which, though a violation of the salt, preservatives, additives, processed and hydrogenated fat rules, were vegan and therefore OK.

Since then, I have to say the diet hasn't been going at all well. Breakfast is impossible, since a) the milkman doesn't deliver soya milk (essential accompaniment to muesli) and b) the children never finish their croissants (butter, jam, blah, blah, blah) and it seems such a waste to throw them away. By the time you've buggered up the morning, you might as well finish off your husband's birthday cake for lunch.

Still, one of the women at my support group recently lost a lot of weight. On Monday night, she died. I'm glad I look well, after all.

E-mail to Carrie, 28 July 1997

Dearest C,

So that's the suspense out the way. Mystic Picardie was
right - CT scan shows I have a brain tumour (the thing they
thought was an infarct a couple of months ago) in my right
front lobe (non-essential part of brain). The liver and lung
disease has worsened ie the taxatere hasn't worked, so I am
stopping chemotherapy. Nothing much left in the treatment
bag: not worth irradiating the head, since my liver will
probably kill me before my brain. So it looks like curtains
this year. Death still seems unreal, since I feel relatively
well. Will be good to have a break from treatment -
steroids, hormones, chemotherapy, bone strengthening, the
lot - for a while. So now I guess it's time for the Gerson
Diet - chemotherapy by vegetables. Yum.

   Did I tell you we are taking the bubbas for baby
bereavement counselling at St Christopher's Hospice. I guess
it will just be playing hospitals, but I'm sure I'm not
telling them enough about what's going on.

   Love from the grim reaper.

   R xxxxx

E-mail to India, 28 July 1997

Dearest India,

Sorry sorry sorry. I have been 'off' e-mail for about a
week. Do you ever get that? The good news is that we aren't
going away this weekend, so please send me address and time
of Oscar's fete. Will he be running the cake stall or
anything? The bad news is that I have just had some more
tests and I heard this pm that I have a brain tumour which I
suspected since I have been getting terrible headaches. Plus
my liver and lung metastases (as we say in the business)
have enlarged which means the chemotherapy isn't working.
Not really anything left in the treatment bag, which means
it's probably curtains this year, which still feels unreal
since I feel relatively well. Anyway, I'm taking a complete

break from treatment - hormones, chemotherapy, steroids, bone strengthening - for at least a month, which will be a relief. Now I will have to go on the mad Gerson anti-cancer diet, which consists of drinking nothing but organic, freshly pressed fruit and vegetables and having coffee enemas on the hour. Lovely. Would you like to join me?

I interviewed Laurence (ne Larry) Fishburne today. Do you think he's sexy? If so, why? V. Ugly in flesh.

Lots of love from the grim reaper xxxx

E-mail from Carrie, 29 July 1997
Dearest R,

No, No, No, No, No, No, No. This can't be happening Ruthie. I don't have the vocabulary for what I felt on receiving your email, but, amongst other emotions, there is a lot of anger, a lot of weeping and a sense of being crushed. How can so much bad news happen to one person? How can modern, alternative and traditional medicine have no effect on this disease? I hate this illness so much. I hate that you will die young, deprive you of your future with your kids and deprive me of my most loyal and loved friend. I hate that you are rendered powerless: that it pulls all the strings and you, Ms-in-control-of-her-life-Picardie, control nothing. I hate that you have put so much into beating this disease and that you get nothing, fucking nothing, in return. I hate the fact that you can't even live the rest of your life in good health. I wish I could say something positive about this horror. But I can't. There is no justice in the world and very obviously no God.

However, I have done some reflection on the issue of J&L's memories of you. I am not saying this to make you feel better. But I think they will remember you. Firstly, I remember before I was 2 - I have memories that nobody would ever have bothered suggesting to me because of their complete banality. Jude, believe it or not, remembers having her nappy changed! So it is possible to have memories from early life (and surely, that's what hypnotherapists rely on). Secondly, you are so central to their little lives that they will ask about you constantly, and be shown photos, and videos and you will be talked about. So memories will be kept alive. Fred remembers people that he has not seen and have not been talked about (and of whom there are no photos) for 7 months. And these people are not a fraction as important to Fred as you are to J&L. I don't think they'll be able to forget you. Is this any comfort? (Of course not. The circumstances don't allow for any comforting.)

Have no heart to send crap trivia (though appreciate the stuff you sent me). Important thing is you mustn't give up and you must live as long and as healthily as possible. From my own selfish standpoint, I don't want to lose you and all you give me a day before I have to. You obviously have reasons of your own why you want to live long and happy. You mustn't be stoical and talk about curtains this year or next. You must stay focussed on the targets. And if you can't do that then you have to pretend you don't have cancer (mmm, no advice as to how you might manage that, but pain relief, adequate rest and good nutrition might make it more difficult to believe you are ill).

The image of the kiddies going to bereavement counselling truly breaks my heart. In fact, the whole damn thing breaks my heart.

Crushed and weeping and wishing you every shred of courage and strength that you need. So utterly sorry that this is happening to you. How inadequate words are.

love, love, xxC

E-mail to Carrie, 30 July 1997
Dearest, bestest Carrie,
Thank you for your wonderful e-mail, which said all the right things. I veer between weeping, feeling totally emotionally and physically drained and being unable to believe I am going to die this year (focus as I might on

goals). I hope to continue e-mailing you from the grave.

It's boiling and sweaty in London, not helped by the appalling hot flushes I am having (not yet eliminated by new, pathetic alternative to Tamoxifen). At least I have slept better for the last two nights, having added Temazepam to my vast stash of drugs. Much better than Mogadon, which makes you feel as if you've been hit over the head by a frying pan. Doesn't make you feel groggy in the morning and I can still get up to pee, attend to children etc. At last I am catching up on two years of sleep deprivation.

Took the kids to lovely under-5s music session in Brockwell Park on Sat morning - they were a bit overawed but had a nice time banging drums. Went to Fire Station near Waterloo with Matt on Sat night and did a lot of crying which was good, because we hardly seem to talk to each other these days. Yummy food, too. Mum wants me to go on the Gerson diet, but I'd never stick to it. And complementary medicine is clearly a load of crap. Afterwards had a joint in the garden, in the cool, with the sky midnight blue. Too much light to see many stars.

Love love love R xxx

E-mail to MClark, 31 July 1997
Dear MClark,
Oh my darling, oh my darling, oh my darling MClark (to be sung to tune of oh my darling Clementine, one of many minor key nursery songs and folk tunes I now sing to my children at bedtime).

Thanks for your hilarious, touching, stellar e-mail. I too keep thinking of the Virgin ad and the grim reaper, but can't face any more treatment (though I might send off for some Native American gunk, having given up the acupuncture and healing, which has transparently failed). Also went to see slightly weird, cadaverous lone gun oncologist on Harley Street who wrote to me via the Obs, who is suggesting more poison. So not yet in zen acceptance.

I am now becoming an internet poetry bore - a friend sent me this poem, In Blackwater Woods, by someone called Mary Oliver:

Every year
Everything
I have ever learned
in my lifetime
leads back to this; the fires
and the black river of loss
whose other side
is salvation, whose meaning
none of us will ever know.
To live in this world
you must be able
to do three things:
to love what is mortal;
to hold it
against your bones knowing
your own life depends on it;
and when the time comes to let it go,
to let it go.

We're on holiday next week. Do you want to come over for supper when we get back? Let's make a date NOW.
Love Roof xxxxx

Letter from reader, 31 July 1997
Dear Ruth,
Since reading your first piece 'Before I Say Goodbye' in the Observer Life magazine a few weeks ago, you've been on my mind so often that I thought I should write. Your words pack no mean punch and leave the reader in no doubt as to the utter horribleness of your illness, but you do so in such a way as to remind us that this is happening to a real flesh-and-blood human being, and not one who has been

mysteriously transformed into some serene apprentice angel with a foot in two worlds. Thanks for hanging on to your albeit darkened sense of humour and for telling us how it is.

Like you, I am 33 and have two small children. I was completely unprepared for the overwhelming, gut-wrenching attachment to one's kids that is a mother's lot, and, when I try to imagine what you're going through, the sheer wrongness of it all makes me so angry and sad that no amount of chocolate/Mr D'Arcy therapy can touch it. (Sorry but George Clooney leaves me cold.)

I feel a bit awkward about writing this because I don't know you, and it's not my style. I also loathe insensitive religious loonies who jump in with all three feet with claims on behalf of the Almighty, but I just wanted to say that I'm praying for you and with an earnestness that surprises me. I struggle with faith, with the apparent randomness of things and with a God who seems to heal some and not others, but I do believe that he can heal people and I'm praying that he'll heal you whether through some miraculous zap, or a more conventional one on the NHS! Anyway, there you go, I've said it.

Please forgive me if this letter is crass or a load of presumptuous cheek - it was simply an impulse I felt I should follow.

Take care.

Yours

Kate Cowell

Nottingham

Observer Life, *3 August 1997*

It's official, then. After nine months of talking bravely about
50:50 survival rates . . . of bone disease being a really 'good'
form of secondary breast cancer . . . of a new, 'natural'
chemotherapy regime which is showing really promising
results . . . of confident declarations of recovery from my
healer and Chinese doctor . . . I now have a brain tumour.
Oh, and, by the way, the lurgy is advancing rapidly into my
liver and lungs, so there's no point in continuing with
treatment. So no more false dawns, no more miracle cures,
no more *Alien*-style eruptions of disease (I now have a 'full
house' of secondary breast cancer sites – or 'mets', as we
professionals like to say). The bottom line is, I'm dying.

Frankly, the brain tumour didn't come as a huge surprise.
I've been getting sicky headaches, lasting three or four days,
and wiggly lights appearing at the periphery of my vision.
Plus, I didn't really believe the doctors back in May, when
they noticed a weird lesion on my brain which, they assured
me, had nothing to do with the breast cancer. Yeah, right,
I've got a rare neurological condition, too.

Still, I'm pretty scared. Not that breast cancer has been a
picnic so far: all those hats I made people buy when I
thought I was going bald and then felt guilty about not
wearing; the fear of getting a new, different cancer from
radiotherapy to the breast (as if!); losing the will to wash the
kitchen floor. Hey, you've heard it all before. But having a
brain tumour is not fun.

My oncologist tells me not to worry, that the right front
lobe is pretty useless, as far as bits of the brain go. Which is
reassuring. Then I read my book – snappily titled *Breast
Cancer* – and it says, 'Secondary tumours in the brain which

produce a rise in pressure within the skull can lead to headaches or to specific neurological signs, such as disorders of speech or movement and epileptic fits. These may also arise from damage by the tumour itself, which can also cause various disorders of mental or nervous system functions, including epilepsy and dementia.' Great. I'm going to die, but I'm going to go bonkers first.

Actually, my oncologist tells me that the liver disease is going to get me before the brain tumour, which is reassuring. 'Secondaries in the liver can cause nausea,' explains my book, 'loss of appetite and weight loss as well as the intense itching and yellow coloration of the skin typical of jaundice . . . Liver tumours which expand rapidly can produce severe pain.' Turning into a bruised lemon is, I reckon, better than going mad.

But whichever bit of my failing anatomy collapses first, I'm pretty upset. What hurts most is losing the future. I won't be there to clap when my beloved babies learn to write their names; I won't see them learn to swim, or go to school, or play the piano; I won't be able to read them *Pippi Longstocking*, or kiss their innocent knees when they fall off their bikes. (All right, so I won't have to clean pooh out of the bath, or watch *Pingu* for the 207th time, or hose spinach sauce off the floor.) Then there's the really important stuff: I won't be able to watch the fourth series of *E R* (will Ross and Hathaway live happily ever after?); I'll never know if the pregnancy stretchmarks on my legs would have disappeared without surgery; I haven't got time to grow my patchy, chemotherapy crop into a halo of life-before-cancer curls.

Plus, there's all the stuff I've got to do now: the agonising task of compiling 'memory boxes' for Lola and Joe (how do you write the definitive love letter to a partly imaginary child?); cleaning out the bathroom cabinet; getting into a size 12.

Meanwhile, it's bloody tough living in limbo, not knowing exactly how long I've got left. Do I get a four-month or a 12-month prescription prepayment certificate? Do I bother stocking up on Sisley day facial scrub, when I've got a whole tube of La Prairie night cleanser left? Can I justify going to the next Ghost sale, and who gets my black skirt after my death?

Still, I'm trying to look on the bright side. Missing the Greenwich Millennium exhibition is not a major source of grief. Matt gets to keep all the guilt if – when push comes to oratory – Lola and Joe end up going to private school (the New Labour Academy of Hypocrisy). And it's one way of solving the post-feminist, double-barrelled, what-surname-to-give-the-kids dilemma. (His. Who wants to be named after a dead post-feminist?)

And, looking back, I don't have many regrets. I was privileged to live through the era of John Frieda restructuring serum, which revolutionised life for women with curly hair. I loved my Matt. We loved our Lola and Joe.

And the future will get on just fine without me. OK, so Matt never waters the garden, which means the wisteria is hardly likely to make the next century. Plus, he never gets up in the night to put blankets back on the kids, but nobody ever died of cold in a centrally heated house. Otherwise, I think life will continue just fine. It's just that I'll miss it so.

Dear Ruth Picardie,

I have just read your article in the Observer and felt I must write to you - don't worry if you are unable to compile memory boxes for your beautiful children - just make sure someone keeps this article for them and they will understand and know what a wonderful person their mother is.

I cannot send my best wishes as your time ahead will not be easy. However I and many other women who read your article will be thinking of you.

Sarah Briggs

London

P.S. You must go to the Ghost sale!

Dear Ruth,

I've just read your article 'Before I Say Goodbye' in the Observer today and feel so moved I must write to you.

My mother died of cancer (ovarian as far as I know) when she was 34 and I was 9 (only child 1965). Please don't stop reading - I expect you receive hundreds of letters like this - it isn't a sob story (well only in part). I want to empathise with your children, adults as they will be, and offer you my humble views on what it is like to be bereaved as a child - and still as an adult.

I didn't attend my mother's funeral - it was seen as somehow 'wrong' or inappropriate at that time - the not so liberated '60s in the North West of England. But it was a day of drama - two cars carrying relatives crashed into each other on the way from Yorkshire and many of them had to spend the day in hospital (the one my mother died in) and missed the funeral. I spent the day at school 'to keep things as normal as possible' I was told later. I tried out a pogo stick for the first time and was allowed the longest 'go' by the headmaster as 'this is a difficult day for Helen'. I can remember taking advantage of my loss many times after this (particularly during the following 3 years spent at boarding school) and still feel guilty about it.

Since my father remarried in 1969 3 years after my mother's death I have had no discussion or conversation with him about my mother, knowing that my stepmother would be offended (she is a difficult woman who married my father when she was 40 and still a virgin) - need I say more? - she still 'believes' that I am her real daughter so at aged 40 I have only just told my own children (2 boys aged 10 and 13) that she is their step grandmother.

My father, with a sigh of relief, handed me over to my new 'mum' and ever since has had any relationship through his wife rather than directly with me and my boys.

My advice (I feel that is too demanding but can't think of another word) is to make sure you continue to be allowed to live after your death - however uncomfortable this may be for your partner and family. Your children are so young that their primary need is for practical and loving care from their father who will not deny your existence and be prepared to answer difficult and unexpected questions later in their lives (such as do I look like my mum?, Did she like opera? Or more recently what is life for?).

I still feel loss that I do not have a 'real' mother but am also aware that I have unwittingly turned her into a paragon of virtue, a perfect version of motherhood - but forever younger than me. Make yourself real in your letters to your children - they will grieve, they must grieve, but by knowing you as a real person, warts and all, it will help their recovery and let you live in them throughout their lives.

Finally, my experience with a stepmother was not the best but it probably allowed me to develop more roundly than grow up 'motherless' - don't put a straitjacket on your partner but make him look carefully before settling and always take his responsibility for his children.

Considering this background I have developed into a reasonable (? I hope) person - I am a dual qualified Speech and Language Therapist and Teacher with a great interest in opera and poetry.

There is life after death.

Yours (and love)

Helen Joy. XX

Great Glen

Letter from reader, 3 August 1997

Dear Ms Picardie,

I haven't stopped thinking about your article since I read it this morning. It stirs so many emotions. For I write from the other side of the fence. I lost my partner last year - a year in three weeks. I can't believe it. At times it seems like an eternity. At others it seems like yesterday. He was 35. I was 34.

The difference in his case was it was sudden. One morning he was there, gaily cycling off to work. The next time I saw him he was dead in the hospital A and E side room. An asthma attack so massive that no wheezer, no amount of ambulance or A and E intervention could save him. Yet he didn't have bad asthma.

So when you said 'what hurts most is losing the future,' I sure know what you mean.

I feel so glad that you had kids. We were still at the talking stage - too many other commitments, him being a student and that. But reading your piece made me realise why, when I see little kids now - and my friends are at that breeding stage - a lump comes into my throat. When your loved one goes, either you want to block it out, or you want to hang onto whatever you can. And memories mean heaps, but it's no way the same as flesh and blood that you can care for, nurture and watch develop.

Anyway, I'm not writing this to burden you - that's the last thing you need. It's the bravery and the wit that shines through your article. That's wonderful.

I don't know what to say about the 'living in limbo' bit.

I often wonder what we'd have done if we had had one more hour, one more day, one more week. If it was just an hour, I'd have held him and held him and held him and held him and cried. Beyond the day mark I think it would have been like a weekend - pottering about, gardening, going to our favourite pub. No great Concorde trips or extravaganzas. Just being with each other.

Your kids will always know what a special mother they had. Scant consolation, I know, for not being there. But life is cruel at times, and there's no point in avoiding that fact. Your memory will stay alive forever, in your Matthew's mind, in that of your friends. Nothing will ever be the same for them. But your love will be ever present. And the tales that everyone tells will build up a picture for your kids. And that will help them. The thought that you want them to be happy - as I know my David wanted me to be - will be the real challenge for your family early on. But reading your article and trying to imagine your family, they will be up to it, even if it takes time. And time is what they have.

So what can I say to close this letter? I wish you strength. Strength to enjoy and cherish the time you have. Courage to throw out boring chores and to just choose to do what you want with who you want. As you have inspired us with your writing, so you will have inspired your family to carry on.

Warmest best wishes
Susanna Harris
Twickenham

Letter from reader, 3 August 1997
Dear Ruth,
I felt compelled to write to you after reading your deeply moving article 'Before I Say Goodbye'.

My son Gary McCallion died at home, on Sunday 29 January 1995. I was holding his hand and talking to him, when he peacefully slipped away. He was 24 years old on 28 December

*1994. Gary had testicular cancer, with secondaries to his
stomach, lungs and finally to his brain. Gary's courage,
dignity and sense of humour, remained intact until the day
he died. What struck me so intensely in your article, was
that you most clearly have those same qualities. It is
surely a privilege for those of us who are so fortunate to
have such wonderful folk in our lives.*

*Please do not think that you will go bonkers. Gary's brain
tumour caused a bit of confusion when he was tired. Once he
tried to make a phone call, he complained that the re-dial
function was not responding. I said 'Gary that is the remote
for your television', we both laughed. Gary said 'you know
me mum, I'm a bit dotty' and I said that he was getting more
like me by the day, we laughed again. He was doing a maths
degree but he thought that he had always been a bit
forgetful. That is honestly as bad as it got.*

*The miracle I prayed for, for Gary, came not in the form
of the cure I so desperately wanted for him. He stayed at
the Bristol Cancer Help Centre for a week. When he came
home, he shared with us that he had found inner peace. He
was also convinced that he was 'coming back'.*

Perhaps the Bristol method could help you too.

*Ruth you will live on through your beautiful children Lola
and Joe, they will never forget you, you do have a future
although it is not what you would have chosen. Everyone who
loves you now, will love you still. Everyone whose lives you
have touched, will feel their lives diminished by your passing.*

Priscilla Hunter

London

Letter from reader, 4 August 1997

Dear Ruth,

*I just thought I'd drop you a line to say that I think your
'Before I Say Goodbye' column is beautifully written, and
that you are fantastically brave and good-humoured – even if
you don't feel it. I've tried to get hold of series 4 of*

*E.R., so you could update yourself on the romantic
shenanigans of gorgeous George and Nurse Hathaway, but, I'm
afraid, it's not yet been delivered to C4. By way of (rather
meagre) consolation, I enclose the feature-length first
episode. I can't bear to watch it, as it merely serves as a
painful reminder that Susan Lewis has abandoned the show
(and therefore me!!). I hope you enjoy it.*

*If there are any other progs from C4 that you'd like me to
lay my hands on, do feel free to contact me. Call it a thank
you for your beautiful writing.*

With my very best wishes,

Benjie Goodhart

Channel 4, London

Letter from reader, 4 August 1997

Dear Ruth Picardie,

*I do hope you will include in your children's memory boxes
your piece in the Observer (3rd August). I imagine that will
give them an insight into your wit, courage, pain and potent
love for them. In addition they will know their mother was a
superb writer who reached the peak of her talent. I am,
myself, in remission from breast cancer. I pray for a
miracle for you (it does happen!). Failing that, lots and
lots of good drugs and all the love you deserve.*

Sending love and light,

Sheila Hancock

London

P. S. Don't even think of replying.

This letter was written in confidence to Ruth and not intended for publication,
although the author has kindly granted permission for its inclusion here.

Letter from reader, 4 August 1997

Dear Ruth,

*I read your piece last night, and again this morning, and it
moves me more than I can say. I had a friend called Hellyn*

65

who had the same range of cancers; when she died (not in great pain) her little girls were 5 and 3. I see them every summer, and although it's sometimes sad to see a look of Hellyn in their faces - I am so glad to go on knowing them and through them, her too.

Your piece is brave and witty, and unbearably sad. Your babies are so young. I cry as I write this - you are all losing so much that you had every right to expect. Is it any good at all, or just irritating, to tell you that when my parents died (together, in a car crash, in October 1992) I became completely certain that they went on in an afterlife - a life I'd never believed in before? Even after nearly 5 years I remember how strongly I felt their spirit with me - it has made me feel far less frightened of death, and I'm writing this in the faint hope of passing on some sense of that certainty to you and to Matt.

With love
Ruth McCarthy
London

Letter from reader, 4 August 1997
Dear Ruth,
Yes there are women with Breast Cancer in this part of the world - judging by the lack of resources available, particularly support groups, drop in centres (and that goes for all Cancer patients), you wouldn't believe it!!

I have your articles pinned on my wall in the office as they keep me going and make me laugh/cry/scream with fear (delete as appropriate). I sent the first one to the local Breast Cancer Nurse - who felt that they would be useful for some 'ladies' (I will kill the next person who calls me a lady). I think that she felt the Observer had somehow become a medical journal and was to be hidden at all costs from anyone who might throw a wobbler if they caught sight of the article. She had obviously forgotten that women with Breast Cancer can read Sunday newspapers without them being vetted.

66

I was diagnosed with 'Inflammatory Breast Cancer' in April this year. This is a rare and 'iffier' type in comparison with the normal (normal????) Breast Cancer. There is a 30-40% chance I might make 5 years - story sound familiar? I am having chemo at the mo so look like a cross between a fat prisoner of war and a plucked chicken - I have disowned my bits 'down below' as they look totally unfamiliar with no hair.

One of the ironies is that I am a manager in the Health Service and used to be a Specialist Nurse in Palliative Care and Cancer Self Help Groups - so everyone in the Cancer service knows me plus I am involved with the development of local Cancer services. So at times it can be really difficult - I can see people that I know going white and clammy when they see me - I've crossed that great professional to patient divide and it confuses everyone including myself.

Anyway - I can hear you snoring. It is great to read your articles - before I was diagnosed I was sick of the Aids sufferers getting first stab at film rights/TV programmes and space in magazines/newspapers. I am hoping to do my bit in good old East Yorkshire - but they are definitely not used to stroppy/challenging/noisy (delete as appropriate) patients here.

I know we shall probably never meet - but I like you am going to rage against the dying of the light. Thank you.

love to you and yours

Yvonne xxx

Hull

PS I've got this thing about Alan Rickman - and I keep imagining meeting him on the train going to the Bristol Cancer Centre - trouble is the chemo hasn't made me a translucent beauty - more of a khaki coloured version of Mr Blobby.

Dear Ruth,

I read your piece in today's Observer and was deeply moved.
It was one of the best bits of journalism I have seen in
years: bitter sweet with black humour and dignity mixed in
just the right proportions. Suffice to say that if I ever
write any 800-worder that is as perfectly crafted, I would
rate it as a fitting tribute in itself. To have done so in
your circumstances is incredible.

This makes this letter all the more difficult to construct.
There is no comment I could possibly make to the substance
of the article, except that - as the father of a
three-year-old boy and three-month girl - it touched a
particularly raw nerve.

No doubt you will not remember, but you were the first girl
I ever kissed. We were in our first or second year at Phil
and Jim and so it must have been about 1969. It was
mid-winter and Justine was playing on the rug in front of
the fire as my father arrived to collect me. While he talked
to your mother, we crept behind the sofa and furtively
embraced. For the next three or four months you were my best
friend. Then we drifted apart, divided by our sex and
probably schools (I think you headed off to the High, while
I went to Bishop Kirk and Abingdon).

Our lives theoretically passed again at Cambridge (I was
at Trinity 1982-5), but we never spoke. Since then I've
watched out for your by-line and always read with interest
and grudging respect (it is always difficult acknowledging
someone with more skill than oneself). Seeing your piece
today prompted me into action, however, and having checked
with Emily Bell that this really was you, I wanted to convey
not so much my sorrow, but my congratulations on what really
was the perfect article.

Please don't bother to reply - you have far more important
things to do with your time - but I hope that the knowledge
of the impression you made today might slightly lift your
spirits.

My love and sympathy,
Daniel Butler
Nantmel, Nr Rhayader

E-mail from India, 5 August 1997

Dearest Ruth,

Major news of the week is that we are definitely moving.
Can't remember if I told you before about massive house in
foul road ... Anyway – we are hoping to get in there by
September, God willing. J very opposed to living in such a
foul road originally, but I've talked him round. But really,
it's the kind of place where people who have nice cars won't
be able to come & visit because their wheels'll get nicked.

I have rediscovered drink in rather a major way recently.
I just love getting slightly drunk. Why is this? I think my
determination to be a chick. So far my two means of
espousing chickdom have been a) lots of drink and b) tons of
makeup. Do you think this is a sort of early-30s crisis? V
good fun, though. Also having lots of dates with safe, ie
totally unattractive but flirtatious, men. Shame I'm still
obese.

My God, what a boring e-mail – like human Mogadon. Will
write interestingly & amusingly tomorrow.

LOTS OF LOVE I xxx

PS Not hugely appropriate in the circs but I must just
tell you this man's last words because it makes me pee with
laughter. He was Ronald Knox, famous 1930s Oxford college
priest, and E Waugh wrote his biography in 1956. Anyway,
Ronald Knox was dying & hadn't said a WORD for weeks.
Someone was sitting with him holding his hand, and the
someone said 'Shall I read to you from the New Testament?',
not expecting a reply, since RK hadn't managed to speak for
ages. But RK suddenly shouted 'NO!' very forcefully. Then he
remembered his manners, and, 'in the idiom of his youth',
according to Waugh, said: 'Awfully jolly of you to suggest
it, though.' And then he died.

Letter from reader, 8 August 1997

Dear Ms Picardie,

I have been deeply moved by your Diary in the Observer. I could go on, but I'll spare you the unsolicited sentimentality of a stranger...

What I did want to say was that I have an abiding image of you in the Guardian Style Section, some years ago wearing the Black Ghost Skirt (cut on the bias?), Birkenstocks and a black jacket, showing how to look cool and happening in that Fashion Wasteland known as 'I've just given birth!'

I've never looked back. (And I've never lost the weight.) Keep on keeping on. Your words speak volumes.

Fiona Smith

Thornton Heath

Observer Life, *10 August 1997*

Since I was diagnosed with cancer last October, I have never a) slept so badly, b) spent so much time at the hairdresser, and c) been so popular. I mean, my address book was fairly full before, but over the past nine months I have been keeping several local florists in business. People I haven't seen for years want to take me out for lunch. The phone never stops ringing.

Obviously, this is very flattering, though Matt complained in November that the kitchen table was looking too funereal. I reckon this is an irrational boy thing, since my friends are too tasteful for carnations. Lunch is my favourite meal of the day (apart from breakfast and tea), so that's been great, if fattening. And it's always good to talk.

But it wasn't always this way. Only last year, a close friend failed to turn up for my birthday dinner. (I got into a mild strop, until my dish of ice-cream arrived.) There were also a few suspicious no-shows for the children's first birthday party; I vowed never to speak to the missing guests again. Dinner invitations were rare, but there were *Friends* and *ER* and lots of, um, quality time at home with Matt.

Then, in October, I got sick. And in between all the mammograms, bone scans, blood tests and chest X-rays, there was a sudden rush of invitations to book launches, weekends away, plays. On Friday, 25 October, I cancelled two lunches, went to a film screening and had dinner at the recently opened and therefore still fashionable Oxo. On Saturday, 2 November, I failed to go to two fireworks displays and a smart 30th birthday party, but managed to rally for lunch the following day. And my new popularity wasn't just a one-month wonder. Only last week I had two lunches (one fashionable), tea (cancelled), one semi-fashionable dinner, and dinner at home in Elephant & Castle (unfashionable) cooked by a friend.

Even total strangers are being amazingly chummy. On a recent cab ride into the West End (how else does a terminally ill girl arrive for lunch?), the driver started oozing – well, I would say flirting, if a slug knew how to flirt – as soon as I sat down. Lived on my own, did I? Lady of leisure, was I? When I eventually went for the subtle approach and said, actually, I was married with two kids, had terminal cancer and, by the way, the hormones and steroids weren't great for the libido (just kidding), my chauffeur got even more excited and started panting, 'Cor! I'd go mad if I were you! No need to worry about Aids or condoms any more!'

Why all this interest in sick people? My experience is wanting to stay as far away from them as possible. For my first dose of chemotherapy, I was put on the medical ward next to an exhausted, elderly lady attached to a tank of oxygen, whose NHS turban kept slipping off her shameful, shiny head. When I was having radiotherapy (every day for six weeks), I kept having appointments at the same time as another elderly lady whose only means of communication appeared to be a very wet cough, facilitated through a tube in her throat. On really bad days, a listless young man would also be in the basement waiting area, wheeled to and from the ward by orderlies wearing rubber aprons and gloves, which I interpreted as cancer plus some God-awful infectious disease. Unfortunately, all this suffering didn't make me feel better about my state of health, or fill me with sympathy for others, but made me feel sick, unheroic and afraid. Mummy, please take it away. (I expect my children will say the same thing, when I am wheezing away in the hospice.)

I can't believe my popularity is simply due to the fact that I'm not yet looking as scary as my fellow patients (though you should see me without pubic hair). Nor can it be my former niceness, which never used to cut it when turning up for birthday dinners. And it certainly isn't the company I presently offer, since terminal illness is like PMT to the power of 10.

A few people, I think, reckon that cripples can help them get to heaven, including my born-again former school teacher who this week sent me a book of 'true life stories of Christians who have all experienced tragedy of one sort or another . . . all of them have found hope in their suffering through knowing the God who suffered first'. In an accompanying letter, she urged me to allow the peace of God into my heart at this difficult time. To her, I say, sorry, Miss, but I was the one who carved '666' on the desks, I'm still half-Jewish (sadly, the wrong half) and no death-bed conversion looms, despite the scary Virgin grim reaper ad.

Worse than the God botherers, though, are the road accident rubber-neckers, who seem to find terminal illness exciting, the secular Samaritans looking for glory. Hey, I met you once three years ago but can we do lunch so I can feel really good about myself when I read your obituary? Yeah, I know we lost touch four years ago, but can I be your best friend again so everyone will feel sorry for me at the funeral?

Enough, already. (Remember what I said about PMT to the power of 10.) I guess most of my friends simply feel desperately sorry for Matt, me and the children and want to help in some small way. And for that I'll always be grateful. Your flowers, letters and cards have made me cry. And the chocolates have sustained me more than I can say.

Dear Ruth Picardie,

Your column in The Observer 'Life' section is the first
article I turn to now on a Sunday morning. They are
wonderful pieces of journalism which must have touched so
many people like me who do not know you.

There are two particular reasons why your articles are so
interesting to me. The first is that a good friend of mine of
very similar age and situation was diagnosed as having
ovarian cancer three and a half years ago. She does not have
a realistic chance of a cure and so during this time I have
tried to see as much of her as possible, knowing that soon I
shall not be able to see her at all. I think this is the
reason why you are suddenly so popular, as you put it -
people who like and love you want to spend as much time with
you as they can, while they can.

The other reason is that I myself have had breast cancer.
I had a mastectomy last March and am currently undergoing
chemotherapy as a prophylactic measure to help prevent
recurrence. The whole thing has been by far the worst
experience of my life but I am not so deserving of sympathy
as you because I have 1) a good chance of a cure; 2) older
children; and 3) lived to 52.

However, you do have a few small (but not trivial) things
to be thankful for. Firstly, unlike me, you have not lost a
breast and your hair. Secondly, your husband is obviously
a 'new man' - your wisteria may not survive but your
children will. Thirdly, unlike me, you are a successful
and accomplished journalist, who writes entertaining,
funny, insightful and clever articles - and so you will
leave much for your children and the world to remember you
by.

If I were a believer, I would certainly pray for you but I
can't even pray for myself. What I wish for you is the same
as for myself - a life, however short or long, that is as
happy as possible and a death, however near or far, that is
peaceful. Try and enjoy whatever you can.

Best wishes
M. H.
London

Letter from reader, 11 August 1997
Dear Ms Picardie,
Over the past few weeks the diary of your experience of
cancer has moved me more than any other piece of writing I
have ever read. I wanted to write to let you know that I am
awed by your honesty and lack of bullshit or bravado. I
intend to use your writings as essential reading for any of
my students embarking on a career in hospice medicine. Since
you seem to have enough chocolate to keep you going I can
only send my thanks for your diary and my best wishes, for
what they are worth, to your family. I, for one, though I
will never meet you, will miss you when you go.
Best wishes
Yours sincerely
Dr Paul Keeley
Glasgow

Observer Life, *17 August 1997*

On the table next to me, collected at random from various
cupboards, are half-empty tumblers of: COQ 10 antioxidant
formula (one tablet to be taken twice a day); emulsified
linseed capsules (three times daily); vitamin C extra (two
tablets twice a day); pycegenol capsules (twice daily) and
mysterious pills initialled WAAC (two tablets daily). Next
to them are glass phials of bone marrow and shark cartilage
(10 drops of each to be taken three times daily). There is also
a packet of potassium and a handful of non-identified
homoeopathic remedies (one of each daily). This, I am
ashamed to admit, is just a small part of the complementary
medicine panic I have been in for the past 10 months.

I started in October by visiting a so-called complementary
guru whom I'm sure won't mind being called Dr Charlatan
(his swish London clinic closed down overnight; he has now
disappeared). First he got me on the aforementioned
supplements, a fraction of which lurk guilty and unfinished
on the table, plus a £275 drink called Yeastone which filled
up half the fridge. Then he got my blood analysed by a
German professor who advised me that refined sugar was
poison and urged me to go on a complicated diet (vinegar
bad, trout good, three-day-old eggs best of all). Finally, he
got me hooked up with a computer expert-cum-homoeopath
for a course of 'Bicom' therapy, which meant being wired up
to a laptop which positively recharged my cells. I think.

All this may sound ridiculous; but when the hospital
baldies have told you, aridly, that such and such a treatment
only has a '50:50 survival benefit', you desperately want to
lengthen the odds. Still, complementary medicine is no
picnic (principally because crisps aren't allowed). I dread to

think how much I spent on Dr Charlatan and friends: his initial quote was £2,500. And even though I turned down his offer of low-level oxygen administration (machine rental £150 per week, consultancy fee £75), plus a five-week course of intravenous injections twice a week, the treatment turned into a huge pressure. By February, I was in such a flap about what pills I should be taking, why I couldn't eat muesli made from raw cereals, and whether or not the Yeastone could be kept in the garden because there was no longer room in the fridge, that I decided to give up the whole thing.

This was, probably, a sensible decision. After all, I'd always been cynical about complementary medicine and the alternative lifestyle, the sort who'd snuck into a tantric yoga class as a sneaky, low-level journalistic trick. I was the woman who had utterly failed her NCT labour (hospital induction, empty birthing pool, four foetal monitors, 20-hour labour, failure to progress beyond 8cm, pethidine, epidural, emergency Caesarean, hospital-induced nervous breakdown). I'm also the person whose athlete's foot has become immune to tea tree oil. What good was alternative healthcare to me?

And yet the panic and desperate hope of a girl with cancer knows no bounds. Friends and family were desperate to help, too: which is why my shelves are groaning with New-Age books: *Sharks Don't Get Cancer*; *Living, Loving and Healing* (written by wise gnome with magic hands); *Full Catastrophe Living* (inspirational picture of high mountain); *Spontaneous Healing* (written by man with beard).

So what did I do? Keep up with the mainstream poison, admit that linseed and books by men with facial hair are not for me? No, silly. I embarked on a weekly Chinese herb and acupuncture regime (£50 a week), which involved wolfing 24 horse tablets a day and drinking as much horrid tea as I could stomach. I persevered for six months, because I once saw Princess Diana leaving the clinic looking thin and chic, so I reckoned I was in good hands.

As if this wasn't enough, I then started going to a healer, first at a group session in London with the vibe of a crematorium (fake flowers on the walls, intergalactic organ in the background). Then I got offered a series of one-on-one appointments at the healer's rural retreat: only £50 plus VAT, crashing New-Age music and a two-hour drive each way. Fun!

Luckily, I have now come to my senses. The expense, the exhausting round of treatment, the sense of failure (I kept forgetting to bring mineral water to be healed; I would 'lose' my Chinese herbs) was part of it. But the thing that finally made me give up on beards was the revelation that complementary medicine does not work! Three months with Dr Charlatan, and the disease had spread to my bones. Six months on Golden Seal Comb and Five Leaf Amachazuru tea, and tumours developed in the liver and lungs. Three months of New-Age bonging, and I ended up with a brain tumour, despite confident declarations from all and sundry that I was on the mend. To be fair to the beards, mainstream treatment from arid white-coats has utterly failed, too, but at least it's a) free, and b) you don't have to listen to Vangelis in hospital.

Luckily, there is a third therapeutic strategy which I am developing almost single-handedly, though sadly not in a controlled trial situation at present, so fellow patients will have to find their own precious path. Essentially, after months of careful research, I have discovered a treatment that is a) cheaper than complementary therapy, b) a hell of a lot more fun than chemotherapy, and c) most important, incredibly effective! Retail therapy! By this, I mean personal indulgence or escapism of any kind. For example, my first breakthrough came when I went to see Daniel Day Lewis and Winona Ryder getting hot and horny in *The Crucible*; during the course of chemotherapy which began the next day, I was sick only once, compared with constant vomiting first time round. Pretty conclusive cause-effect, no? Soon after, I spent the morning having a divine Jurlique facial and the afternoon at the Ghost warehouse sale: the following day, my blood count was completely normal.

Then came my major shopping breakthrough: a long consultation at the Dickins & Jones personal beauty studio with skincare god John Gustafson. Perhaps the most important retail oncologist in the country, he has evolved a stellar personal skin regime based on these rare products: Sisley, La Prairie, Shiseido, Elizabeth Arden, Bobbi Brown and Prescriptives. For just £250, I started looking like a film star (compared with £250 for vile Yeastone, which ended up down the sink), despite being two-thirds through the chemotherapy course from hell.

Thanks to this highly evolved, only moderately expensive and largely side-effect-free treatment (warning: my credit card bounced earlier today), I am currently in almost no pain! My symptoms are a slightly swollen brain, but I'm hoping that today's lunch (smoked salmon bagels, crisps, extra French dressing) will have a positive effect. The other problem – my enlarged liver – I believe has been solved by my later splurge at Whistles sale (blue skirt, lilac shirt). Even if the dread organ doesn't shrink, the clever bias cutting hides most of the lumps.

So have hope, fellow cripples. My non-beard book, *Shop Yourself out of Cancer*, is coming soon.

Letter from reader, 17 August 1997

Dear Ruth,

I am writing this from the Bristol Travel Lodge where I am staying for one night before spending a week at the Bristol Cancer Centre. I have just been diagnosed as having a breast cancer which is moving faster than Linford Christie on a good day. I immediately set out to find Dr Charlatan.

Thank you so much for your article and/or being so humorous and courageous. I read it in a service station on the way here and burst out laughing several times, something I haven't done for quite some time.

If we don't meet this time around I sure as hell hope we do the next time.

Love and best wishes
Jackie Liversey
Accrington

Letter from reader, 21 August 1997

Dear Ruth,

I was so moved by your frank and amusing article in Life recently, that I felt I had to write and impart my experience as one of the 'deserted survivors' that may offer some solace to you or your family.

I am 25, a Recruitment Consultant at Graduate Appointments – a job I fell into after graduating and failing to secure a creative position in the ever competitive 'media' industry. I think my father would be proud – that I have a 'good' job and have not become a bum and have hopefully retained the integrity, moral values and consideration for others that he instilled in me.

I was eighteen and in my first year of UCL when Dad was first spirited off to hospital under mysterious circumstances. My mother phoned me in my hall of residence to tell me he was having a 'routine' operation. He had wanted to keep the distressing news from my sister and I. In actuality, he had undergone a highly dangerous operation to remove most of his

cancer-ridden oesophagus and some of his stomach which was
then moved into his chest cavity. I do not wish to dwell on
the geography and particulars of what was to become known as
'the beast', which will be of little interest to you.

My father was a GP (in an ironic twist that was not lost
on him). He was based in a small practice in Harrow. How to
describe him ... to you a faceless stranger? He was
considerably older than my mother (by eighteen years) when he
first invited her to do a run with him on an Austrian ski slope
where they first met. However, he was youthful and energetic
with laughing eyes that displayed compassion but severity at
the same time. He was many men - a first-class sailor, a mentor,
a top-scoring Scrabble player, an ever compassionate, patient
doctor, an erratic tennis player with a hilarious serve with
which he would invariably win during family doubles while we
guffawed and snorted helplessly ... but most of all he was
a selfless family man who was loved and respected by all that
met him. He adored us, the kids and my mother. At the same time,
he never suffered fools and was intolerant of superficiality. He
would never pretend to like people that he despised.

He knew more than anyone that he was now living on
borrowed time. His first tumour revealed an extremely rare
but fiercely malignant cancer that would probably be back for
a second instalment. So we enjoyed ourselves. We
relinquished the family sized tent of numerous camping
holidays of happy years past, and booked a flotilla holiday
in the Sporades - my younger sister, Peta, was also present.

It was a marvellous tonic. He was doing what he loved. Even
then, though, he was displaying uncharacteristic mood swings
and a short fuse that we had rarely witnessed in 'pre-beast'
times. My mother and he threw plates and danced like newly-
weds providing me with comforting, mental snapshots now.

Life continued much the same as usual. I led a typical
student existence while my sister embarked on four 'A'
levels. Although it was rarely mentioned we all felt dread
for the future.

One day, about two years after the original tumour had

been diagnosed, Dad came home early from work saying he had been unable to write out a prescription. He had brain mets ... And yes it was probably terminal. The timing was awful - I was just about to go to Italy for my 3rd year and was thrown into a crisis. I decided eventually to take a year off and so commenced our long and harsh journey.

During his treatment, I was alone with him while my Mum worked and my sister studied. It was both a distressing and soul-searching period. Ironically, time having run out, there was so much time for me to get to know him for he had never been a man of frivolous words. The knowledge of our eventual separation made the laughter harder and the words sincerer. I composed a letter to him thanking him for being such an inspirational father and telling him how much I loved him as the tension and perpetual lump in the throat prevented me from telling him in conversation.

Over these months I noticed a change in Dad. He went from a dwindling shadow of a man who would often crumple in my arms, with shuddering sobs as we talked about our feelings, to having a certain fortitude and calm acceptance of his situation. In the months approaching his death - we even began to joke. One day, I came into the bathroom to see him splashing on aftershave as if he was washing in the stuff.

'Dad, aren't you overdoing it a bit?'

'It's very expensive this stuff you know - I'm hoping to finish it before I kick the bucket.'

On another occasion, we talked quite frankly and Dad said how unafraid he was of dying ... he just wanted to look after 'his girls' though. He'd had a good innings, had a wonderful family etc.

When his time came, it was in a grotty NHS ward rather than at home. The day he died - a Monday evening in June 1993 - was gloomy, torrential rain bounced off the pavements in glassy rods as I ran from the tube to his bedside. I hadn't known he had suddenly become ill over the weekend with a blood clot as I had spent the weekend with friends in Norfolk where I sat in an eerily peaceful, vast poppy field. Dad was due to come home the

*following week. I came to the hospital full of self
recriminations for having ever strayed from the hospital. This
was it, I tried to tell him I was sorry, taking his already
lifeless hand in mine as he slipped in and out of
consciousness. I don't know if he was still lucid.*

*Two weeks after he died I met him in a dream in which I
got out of bed and went downstairs, knowing as I did so that
if I went into the living room (which had french windows) I
would see him through the windows gardening. He was. He
looked up from his work and came over to the window. We
placed our palms together on opposite sides of the glass. I
said 'I love you Dad'. He replied 'I know'. I asked 'Will I
ever see you again?' to which he said 'Of course you will'.
The glass separating our two worlds disappeared and I woke
up in tears of happiness.*

*Four years on his girls are doing alright. We have
survived his death ... when I can remember feeling that I
couldn't possibly go on without him, when I'd cried so much
there was no more white in my eyes to be seen. I don't love
him any less. The vast hole that was left by his death is
gradually growing back together like a well-stitched wound.
It is not the end of the world after all – we are all
terminally ill. Billions have died over the years ... how
hard can it be? He, as I believe everyone does, only died
when he was ready to. He gave the final green light when he
stopped being able to do the things he wanted and was
beginning the slide into indignity and helplessness.*

*I didn't mean this letter to be so long. I am sure you
will have had many. I hope it hasn't distressed you.
Whatever possessed Life to put your words amongst the
banality of the TV guide?*

*I wish you the best for your dying. I hope it is painless
and that your family surround you and help you. You would be
in my prayers if I wasn't atheist.*

Best wishes to you and your family.
Alix Miller
London

Observer Life, *24 August 1997*

As every pop-psychologist knows, denial is the first stage of coming to terms with death. 'Among the over 200 dying patients we have interviewed,' writes Elisabeth Kubler-Ross in her classic work *On Death and Dying*, 'most reacted to the awareness of a terminal illness at first with the statement, "No, not me, it cannot be true." ' Apparently, patients then move on, over a period of months, to anger, bargaining, depression and finally acceptance.

Me? I used to think I was a fast-track kind of girl, the sort who began a diet on a Monday (muesli for breakfast); stuck to it really well until Wednesday (baked potato, no butter for lunch); accidentally ate some garlic bread with a bowl of low-calorie gazpacho on Thursday; decided on Saturday that a bowl of raspberries (fresh, unlimited) couldn't really be eaten without a small tub of cream (M&S extra thick); and by Sunday realised that, actually, calorie-counting put your metabolism in starvation mode. Months? Pooey. I used to be the sort of superwoman who spent a mere week moving through the five well-known stages of coming to terms with having a spare tyre: depression, anger, bargaining, denial, acceptance. What else do you expect from an evolved, post-feminist chick?

Sadly, being diagnosed with cancer seems to have arrested my capacity for high-powered psychological evolution. For – a shocking 10 months since Diagnosis Day – I have become convinced that I am, in fact, pregnant. Which, on the face of it, is down there in the kindergarten of denial, or possibly the mania of bargaining, or at the very best the delusion of depression.

However, I need only to refer you to one of the pregnancy

manuals dusting up my shelves: the vomiting, the weird stuff growing inside you, the endless waiting for the big day.

This is where Ruth's column ends, though it is not the ending she intended, *writes her sister, Justine Picardie*. She is now in a hospice, too ill to finish this article, though I think I know what she intended to say. Her twins, Lola and Joe, were born two years ago this week. The similarity between those hot August days before she gave birth, and now, is perhaps not as far-fetched as it seems. Friends telephone, wanting to know the news, though there is nothing yet to tell; flowers arrive, as if in anticipation; the sticky afternoons drift by; the nights seem to last forever.

But unlike two years ago, there is no fixed due date. There have been times in the past few days when Ruth has fallen asleep in her hospital bed, and I've wondered if she will ever wake up again. Then she opens her eyes, and ruminatively eats another chocolate biscuit. She has talked about leaving the hospice in time for Lola and Joe's birthday party, about future shopping expeditions and trips to the theatre, about writing another column.

So this is not a neat conclusion, nor even rough prediction of what to expect next. Last Sunday, I sat with Ruth in the hospice, and she added a handwritten note to the bottom of her unfinished column. 'So here I am, still waiting for the big day which I hope and half-hope won't come. Will keep you posted!'

Dear Ruth,

*After I read one of your earlier columns, I got on the
internet to find some advice on how to examine breasts.*

*I printed it and gave it to Susy, my girlfriend, and I
will make sure that she follows the instructions.*

*This might seem like a strange thing to be writing to you
at this time, but you made me do it. You made me lie awake
one night and just watch her sleep and realise how amazingly
fragile and precious she was. You made me wake up to the
awful possibility of loss.*

*This is what you have added to my life and the lives of
all the other men you touched with your words.*

I believe in God and I know that my God is with you.
Anonymous

Darling One,

Anyway, my desperate cyber silence is due to a bout of
madness. My god, your amazing cake arrived three seconds
ago! It is the most beautiful thing I have ever seen in my
whole life and will last all of supper time. Thank you,
thank you, thank you. Now you will starve all week.

Wish I could get into drinking: am on sleeping tablets, which
make you feel far worse in the morning. Groggy until four pints
of strong coffee have given you a horrid time on the loo.

J Guf sent me some replacement facial regime freebies -
what a honey. Having my eyebrows sheared again on 12th.

love from another human mogadon.

r xxxxx

Dearest Annette,

Thank you for the beautiful poems - as if I could add to the
canon on the internet! But I would love to read some more Primo

Levi (or Anne Frank?) poetry in particular - I didn't realise
he'd written any. Am particularly interested in how holocaust
victims contemplated death (she said melodramatically).

Meanwhile, tired and addled by drugs docs are obsessed
with filling me with - tranquillisers at the moment (why not
sleeping tablets, which is what I want?). I am as anti
conventional and complementary medicine as ever, and why not
- they've all fucked up so far. Shopping and eating is the
only therapy that works.

The babes' birthday was lovely, albeit scaled down. We had
our wedding caterer and a Jewish birthday blessing from Dad
and Peggy Seeger and Neill singing the First Time Ever I Saw
Your Face, so lots of tears and happy times revisited. L&J
now have so many presents it's obscene - they must not get
any more birthday presents at all.

The Gower was fab, too, though started going a bit bonkers
and having Prozac-induced panic attacks in the supermarket.
But lovely weather to begin with for long walks on beach and
shell collecting and wild flowers and butterflies and sunsets.
Then cloudy but perfect for all day barbecue on the beach
with burnt marshmallows and hot dogs. Felt very strong for
long walks but now very hard walking upstairs. Why?

All love to you. Are you strong? Let me know.

Ruthie xxxxx

E-mail to Carrie, 2 September 1997
Dearest C,
Britain in mourning for you know who - does anybody care in
Vietnam about the death of the media's golden goose? I found
out at 6am, told by a distraught visitor at hospice. I have to
say I shed a tear for the icon - if she can go at 36 why not me at
33 (actually that's a tear for me, of course). Flowers can't be
bought in London, apparently, and everyone is in black.

Anyway, I'm writing this in a brief moment of non-fuggy
lucidity. Glad (another) journey from hell is over (again).
I am so fat at the moment - the steroids make me look like I

have a goitre and my liver is so puffed up I could be four
(?) months pregnant at least.

Have been sleeping at the hospice, where the food is
disgusting, so getting heavily into M&S take away salad and
Pret A Manger sandwiches. They want to put me on huge doses
of tranquillisers day and night for some reason - why are
doctors obsessed with drugs? (Deals with drug companies.)
Also on huge quantities of fattening steroids. The children
have an obscene number of toys. They must never have any
again. And on that acid note . . .

E-mail working again, hooray. Not.

Love love love Ruthie xxx

E-mail to India, 4 September 1997
Dearest India,
At last a reply to your 8 million e-mails. Expect extremely
low levels of wit and length.

PLEASE visit me at hospice, where they are very nice but
food is disgusting (supper: tinned spaghetti, inedible
potato croquettes, veg burger only just bearable if swathed
in ketchup) so you must always bring pret a manger
sandwiches. I am the youngest person here by about 50 years.
Beautiful garden, open to the public four times a year. I am
being very stroppy with doctor about drugs.

You must write the Bloomsbury biography - you are a
brilliant writer and there are no good subjects left. And
why haven't you told me about your play?

So glad you are drinking like a fish - slightly worried you
were going to have eight children.

Panicking slightly over winter wardrobe. Any good shoes/
clothes in M&S? Ghost don't seem to like winter.

So what do you feel about Di? I shed a tear, after being
the first person in the world to hear (told by distraught
visitor to hospice at 6am). The big question is what's the
British fashion industry going to do?

I love you very much. Ruthie xxxxxx

E-mail to India, 11 September 1997

dearest i

sorry about lunch today and not seeing my new eyebrows and
face lift. i get so very tired and seem to manage only one
thing a day. my sister gave me a massage and i am going to a
george clooney action blow-out tonight. have you seen stork?
butch eighties fashion and stupid piece on why wales is the
new rock n roll, ho ho. have you seen brilliant new movie
full monty? sheffield is new seattle for disenfranchised man,
you'd think wagadon could get it together, they should have
given the job to you. mirabella disaster i reckon all over
again. are you going to the party. also conde nast
traveller, you should be writing for it.

 i will need a wheelchair soon. lovely and glamorous. also
morphine. ever had any? we are going to cork in a couple of
weekends. also trying for day trips to oxford and cambridge.
after that i reckon i haven't got long. just fed up with the
whole struggle. but plenty of time for e-mails and chocolate
cake before then. don't forget lots of john g at the funeral
and ethnic input all round.

 all love ruthie xxx

E-mail to Jamie, 12 September 1997

darling jamie,

sorry i've been so out of touch. i feel close to the end now,
more or less living in my bedroom with handy en suite bathroom.
i haven't had a bath for about a week and really smell. but i
want to see your flat before i go, she said melodramatically.
what films would you like to see? something crass please
followed by not poons.

 love you lots
 remember you're going to be an e-mail star
 ruthie xxx

E-mail to Carrie, 12 September 1997

darling carrie,

thanks for your stash of e-mails. i feel close to the end
now - weary and in pain. maybe i'll make the first
anniversary of my diagnosis in october. we'll let you know
if d-day seems to be approaching and you can double up for
the funeral too - probably steyning, though i just want a
stone the kids can visit. the summer has gone very quickly.
anyway, i've checked out of the hospice (they gave lola a
fluffy toucan) and am more or less living in the bedroom with
handy en suite bathroom. my legs are very weak so getting up
and out is a real effort - i haven't had a bath for a week
and really smell. matt has gone to get a wheelchair which
should make things easier and it might be time for morphine.
hardly do anything with the kids - guilt, guilt - but they've
had two years. anyway, treats still planned, like trip to
cambridge tomorrow with jenny and simon and charlie and leanne
to see steves. haven't been there for years, literally. hoping
for slanting sun on the backs. last night j, l and i went to see
gloriously silly george clooney action movie followed by
chinese food at poons. we are also going to ireland next
weekend to stay at amazing ballymaloe court.

steroids making my face moon like. a marrying woman with
8-year-old son. d's 44-year-old girlfriend just had an
abortion. l and c trying for a baby. ditto j who has finally
stopped breastfeeding completely and is in boob agony.

love you lots r xxxxxxxxxx

Letter from Jenny Dee, 18 September 1997

Dearest Ruthie,

*You are my best friend and I am so reluctant to let you go.
I've been putting off thinking about you dying because I
just don't know how my life will be without you. We have
done so many hugely important and amazingly trivial things
together - you are the diary that I never kept. The language
of love and loss seems so inept at the moment. All I can say*

is that I will miss you forever, you are my best friend forever and I love you forever. I promise to love Matt and Joe and Lola and, in particular, take care of the parts of them that are you. I am so sad but also delighted that I have known you for 33 years.

Big love, Jenny X

Observer Life, *28 September 1997*

My sister, Ruth Picardie, died this week, in the early hours of Monday morning. I know there are many readers who will want to be told about this, because in the short time that Ruth wrote a column for *Life*, she generated a huge number of letters. After her column stopped, somewhat abruptly, when she was too ill to go on, even more letters arrived: hundreds and hundreds of them, all asking what happened next.

Well, here is a little bit of what happened next. Ruth, who was diagnosed with breast cancer last October at the age of 32, has already described the rapid spread of the disease: to her lymph, her bones, her liver, her lungs and, finally, her brain. She had predicted, wryly, that she would 'turn the colour of a bruised lemon and go bonkers'; and in fact a few weeks ago, the brain tumours did make her quite mad. She raged in a hospital bed, while the doctors looked embarrassed at their failure to save her, and was then moved to a hospice. But slowly, after an unwilling stint among the dying, Ruth seemed to claw her way back to life: in time to return home and celebrate her twins' second birthday at the end of August with chocolate cake and Champagne; in time to have her own brief Indian summer.

True, she was by now confined to a wheelchair, and very weak; but still she seized hold of the big things she loved in life: her children, her family, her friends; and also the small things that make people happy yet are too often forgotten: the colour of a bright lipstick, the scent of late-flowering sweet peas, the pleasure of a newly-planted pot of lavender.

Less than a fortnight before she died, she made an expedition into the centre of London: to buy some fabulous face cream and to have her eyebrows shaped. A few days later, she came to a picnic in the park for my son's eighth birthday. She ate birthday cake and prawn sandwiches and the children rode gaily in the wheelchair with her. We talked about her plans for a weekend away in Ireland, about next year's summer holidays, about her children's third birthday, about her writing a book.

Instead, last Sunday, Ruth became very, very ill: unable to breathe without oxygen, choked by the obscene tumours that had invaded every part of her brave body. She was racked with pain, and returned in an ambulance to the hospice that had nursed her in previous crises. She had pulled through before, inexorable in her determination to go on living, and I expected her to recover again: to open her eyes and ask for a cup of cocoa or a chocolate biscuit; to demand to be taken home or out to lunch or to a party: somewhere, anywhere, more interesting.

But somehow, Ruth slipped away to a different place, a place where I could not go with her. It seems impossible: impossible to comprehend; impossible to find the words to describe the loss. After she died, I sat with her body, stroking her face, holding her hand. She was cold, and my hand could not warm her hand, but I could not believe that she had stopped breathing: even at the end, she had still been so full of life.

Her face looked peaceful; though her eyebrows were raised in a slightly quizzical manner: as if to say, how can this be?

Justine Picardie

Aug 97

Dearest, darling, best boy Ore,

I will love you forever and a day. You are nearly two and the sweetest boy in the whole world. You look like an angel. Suck your thumb. Learning to talk beautifully. Love riding your bike and your tiger plug. Bit naughty going to bed! You are the best thing that ever happened to me and Daddy and the hardest thing to let go. Daddy loves you so much. So do granny + grandad (both), Justine, Lizzie. Ask them about me, beautiful boy. Be happy.

　　　　xx MOMMY xx

You love soldiers!

You are as musical as an angel! You sing like an angel! Always enjoy your music — I played piano (grade 7 failed) and cello. String quartet and orchestras.

You love saying "Oh dear" and "Be careful." Worried about stones on beach! You love animals specially horses!

Aug 1997

Dearest Lola, best girl, beauty,

I love you. You are nearly two and fabulous. So intelligent, beautiful, independent, feisty, strong but cuddly + soft, too. I'll always love you, even though I'm not there physically. Daddy loves you, Justine loves you, Joe loves you, granny + grandad (all of them) love you. You were the best thing that ever happened to me and daddy and letting you go the hardest. Be yourself my baby girl.

X X X X MUMMY

PS You look just like me. Hooray! Ask all your relatives and Daddy's friends (Jenny, Carrie, Steves, Charlie, Leanne etc) for more info about me!

Blue is your favourite colour!
You love ladybirds!
You love nanny's African lullaby!
You love clothes! Same here! Your godmother, Big Lola will take you shopping at Harvey Nicks. So will Joe's godmother, Lizzie!

After Words by Matt Seaton

By the time she had reached her early thirties, you could say that Ruth Picardie was a journalist to her essential core. Not in the snide sense that she was a 'hack', but that she was an exceptionally versatile writer – one for whom all life experiences were grist to the mill of her sensibility: clothes, movies, motherhood, it was all there.

It was a very Ruth thing to do to write about her cancer in the way she did. Her disarming candour and mordant wit, a crisply vernacular style and an unerring instinct for the emotional truth of a situation, were the qualities her friends loved her for – and they were what her readers valued too. There was no discernible difference between the voice Ruth found as a writer in her 'Before I Say Goodbye' columns and the voice she spoke in. That, I think, is why so many people responded to reading about her terminal illness with such unprecedented feeling. She touched and moved people because they felt they knew her simply through her writing. It was true; they did. And they cared.

More importantly, she showed that it was possible to face one's worst fears and laugh, to live fully and deeply if too briefly, and not to be snuffed out submissively but to blaze away until the last possible moment. If she could, she would have written more: it was in her mind that this work would make a book, and it was perhaps the only real disappointment of her career that she felt she'd left this undone. Except that here we are, and her ambition has been realised after all.

But where does that leave me, the husband and parent left behind? What claim have I to write here? A more modest one, certainly: I started what I originally wrote for *Observer Life* simply because I wanted to inform people about what had happened in Ruth's last weeks when she had no longer been able to write herself. I knew I couldn't emulate her style and her particular gift for phrase-making, even for an instant, but I felt that at least I could show how Ruth went on being her glorious bolshy, spirited self until the day death finally overtook her.

But, of course, as the piece took shape, I realised I had my own reasons for writing. I wrote partly as therapy, perhaps, and one or two people who've been through similar trials have said, kindly but with real feeling, that they envied me the opportunity that I had, to write and be published. It is, I acknowledge, an extraordinary privilege – and not one to be squandered by a self-indulgent parading of private sorrow.

I hope that is not what I do; or if it is partly true, then that there is some redeeming purpose besides. What I wanted to achieve was to describe, in as clear-eyed a way as I knew how, the pain of losing someone dear in all its messy ambivalence. In the days that followed Ruth's death, I received two copies of C. S. Lewis's *A Grief Observed* – one from a friend, another from a total stranger who had read the *Observer* and wrote, with great generosity, from similar circumstances. Although the passages in which Lewis wrestles with his Christian faith seem now of minoritarian interest, it remains a marvellous short book, all the better for having been written simply as a notebook hardly intended for publication and thus possessing an unvarnished, almost artless honesty. Without doubt, over the years, it has been a comfort and a crutch to tens, probably hundreds of thousands, of the bereaved.

Nothing I could write would ever bear comparison to Lewis's little masterpiece, but I felt that if I could extend the work of Ruth's writing about breast cancer by writing about death and loss, then there might be something truthful that could possibly be of use to somebody somewhere – a glimmer of recognition here, the pleasure of finding something previously felt but not previously named there.

Apart, it goes without saying, from our children, perhaps

the one good thing I have got out of all this grief is that I have shed a little of the cynicism that so often seems to come as standard issue with a press card, and discovered that words matter – not just the articles published in newspapers and magazines, but the letters written by friends and strangers alike: words of eloquent sympathy and speaking sorrow. Words were Ruth's element, but they belong to us all.

'Great! I'm going to die of cancer,' wrote Ruth in one of her last columns, 'but I'm going to go bonkers first.' There was a rough-tough bravado about Ruth's black humour: it was a way not so much of facing the truth, as of trying to face it down; a means of both acknowledging the inevitable and denying it, in a shriek of raucous laughter.

That was Ruth's way of dealing with a predicament that was, most of the time, too big and too fearful for any of us properly to comprehend. All year there was a deep sense of unreality about how serious her illness was: until just a few weeks before she died, she looked – apart from her unaccustomed crop – much as she had ever done.

Some of the time, in fact, thanks to a newly discovered faith in the efficacy of some very expensive facial products, she looked better than ever. Some people believe in the power of prayer; Ruth believed in the power of vitamin-enriched, anti-ageing moisturiser.

Paradoxically, it was only during treatment, the drearily prolonged bouts of chemo, that she was really laid low. Then, all of a sudden, there was no getting round it: we were living with someone with a serious illness. Mummy's sick, we used to tell the children. Mummy has to have medicine, and that makes her sick, though it might make her well again. Except even that crooked logic – so counterintuitive, one felt, that it *must* be true – fell through in the end.

But as much as Ruth's capital-A attitude was a way of both defying and accepting her cancer, it was also a piece of performance for our benefit. If there was one thing she couldn't stand, it was people hanging around with long faces, feeling terrible and not knowing what to say. Before she became too ill to care, Ruth was hilariously impatient with people she felt were inadequate in dealing with the fact that she had cancer.

Always a great compiler of lists – it was one of her ways of organising the world, but also an enjoyable little neurosis she allowed herself – she started and discarded several mini-ledgers of those who were to be banned from her funeral on the grounds of failing the 'cancer victim' test. At one stage, I think there may even have been an A-list of absolute untouchables and a B-list of probationaries – though a gift of chocolate or flowers (provided they were anything other than carnations) was probably enough to have got you off either.

I understood her exasperation, but I knew from experience that it wasn't always easy to judge the mood. Sometimes Ruth would be furious with people for ignoring the C-word and just gossiping about the everyday; at other times, she'd declare herself sick of the subject and wish people wouldn't drone on and on about such-and-such a new treatment they'd read about in a magazine at the dentist's, or what their aunt had done when she was diagnosed.

There was no right way for any of us. If I learnt one thing over Ruth's last weeks, it was that the illusions one holds about a peaceful, dignified death and the family's perfect bedside farewell will almost certainly be tugged away. If one is left with any shreds of comfort, then they must be unlooked-for blessings. Dying is nasty, ugly and painful; it's so obvious, isn't it?

Ruth and I were constitutionally optimistic types. Maybe we believed a little too much in our luck, that we somehow deserved a providentially good life. Without strenuous effort or fervent ambition, things seemed always to fall more or less into place. Until, that is, we tried to have children. For two years we tried and, for no reason that doctors could find, failed to conceive. I'd always blithely assumed we would have children sometime, but gradually our track record of increasingly non-recreational sex began to tell against the likelihood of that eventuality. Then, suddenly, we were dealt the most fantastic backslap of good fortune: Ruth became pregnant with twins at our first attempt of IVF. Perfect! Two at once, a boy and a girl – the instant family.

Pregnancy was an ordeal for Ruth; there's no other way she would have allowed me to describe it. She was sick for four months. Morning sickness, in her case, was a complete misnomer: she would wake up, be sick; have some toast for breakfast and go to work, be sick when she got there; force herself to have some lunch, be sick again; come home, be sick and go to bed. We both became so used to her retching that, after a while, it was just part of the daily routine, barely worthy of comment.

And then, almost as soon as she started feeling less nauseous, she seemed to become enormous – that vast swelling belly rendering her entire pre-pregnancy wardrobe laughably obsolete. But I was vastly proud of her, too. And, although this may be just horribly conceited of me, I felt there was a characteristic largesse in our having twins. It spoke of a generosity – and a greediness – that was true to her, and to us both. She would never do things by halves, or even single portions. Seconds, please – let's have a double!

Despite her gruesome spell of morning-noon-and-night sickness, Ruth eventually emerged with her self-reliance and sense of mischief intact. On holiday in Greece in May 1995, when she was nearly six months pregnant and her tummy was already ballooning into cartoonish proportions, she scandalised the local populace by riding a mountain bike round the island. Even though she huffed and puffed, and had to stop in the shade every half-mile or so, she enjoyed the fuss enormously.

But as that long hot summer went on, the physical strain of pregnancy taxed her hard. Once, as she was walking near our house a few weeks after that holiday, Ruth stumbled and fell – her centre of gravity all awry. Feeling nauseous with pain – since, though she didn't yet know it, she had broken a bone in her foot – she managed to hail a cab, literally crawl into it and beg to be taken to casualty.

Perhaps this is fanciful hindsight, but I sometimes feel that the arduous experience of her twin pregnancy taught her, if almost imperceptibly, to mistrust her body, to feel that it was not the constant, easy friend it had been. She used to say herself that she felt the foetuses she was carrying were somehow inimical to her – as if they were parasitical aliens like the Midwich Cuckoos. It had nothing to do with how she felt about having children; about that she was unambivalently positive. It was simply how she chose to describe the physical sensation of being pregnant.

If Ruth did fall out of love with her body, then perhaps it had been so gradual a process, predating her cancer, that she did not fully recognise it. Pregnancy was laborious to her, in every sense; birth, ultimately by Caesarean, a trauma; and breastfeeding a trial. All those physical metamorphoses and hormonal mutations, I think, threw into disarray that delicate sense of being in control of her body and its destiny. There had been a subtle alienation there – even before cancer was diagnosed, a couple of months after the twins' first birthday.

And the cancer, when it came, made that phantom sense of malaise all too real and palpable. Cancer is always cruel, but cancer of the breast contains an especially sour little irony. The breast, symbol of everything maternal, a source of life-sustaining human milk, guarantor of new-born babies' immunity from disease – that, for one woman in twelve, the breast should harbour the seed of her destruction seems like a crudely misogynist practical joke.

If I close my eyes and travel in time, I can still feel the delicious weight of Ruth's left breast in my right hand. Eros and, as it turned out, Thanatos gorgeously cupped in my palm. That was before we knew about her cancer. Once we knew, I found it unbearable to touch her there. She never seemed to blame my squeamishness, but in retrospect the lump not only grew within her, but between us, spreading, as inexorably as the cancer itself did.

Small wonder cancer has held so much appeal to writers and poets as a metaphor for social corrosion and political alienation: it goes about its grim business on many levels. In the last few weeks, when the cancer was rapidly advancing towards the ultimate Pyrrhic victory of killing its host, I often felt that, as Ruth was dying, our relationship was by degrees dying with her.

You always imagine death as a sudden event, a clean break between being and non-being, possession and loss – and for some, facing perhaps the dreadful trauma of losing a loved one killed suddenly in an accident, that is how it must be. But with a progressive disease like cancer, dying is a relentlessly attritional process of estrangement. You want so much to do and say the right thing, but you are doomed to frustration, failure and regret. The only really 'right thing' would be to make that person you love well again, and that is the one great godlike task you cannot perform.

I know I was wrong in many important ways: our relationship is an irreducible historical fact – for eleven years, before the cancer, it was what it was, and nothing can alter that. And it lives on, too, in the most real possible way in our children; there is no greater saving grace.

I know also that regret and guilt are the classic symptoms of bereavement. In a sense, I'm aware that what I feel is almost a cliché. None of that, though, alters the angrily chafing, subjective truth of the feeling. I just wish – how I wish – I could have somehow got round it: loved Ruth, or made her feel loved, in the old way, to the very end.

But the truth is that it was no longer possible. The cancer had interpolated itself, sending out its rogue cells to multiply madly and lay waste like an army of termites. Cancer changed everything: it put us on different tracks, stretching our grasp of one another to the limit and eventually forcing us apart. In the end, I could not reach her, and it felt like a failure in me. And then she was gone.

Because Ruth had been told that her lump was harmless two years earlier, we'd both been blasé when it had clearly started to grow. The fool's paradise of complacency that – unwittingly – we'd been living in meant that I didn't even go with her when she went back for the results of her second round of tests in October 1996.

She called me at work from a payphone at the hospital, distraught, in tears, barely able to get the words out: 'It's cancer. I've got cancer.' The sensation of that moment is etched on my psyche like scar tissue. Suddenly, the desk I was leaning on seemed to plummet away from me vertiginously. I felt hot and then instantly cold; my brain felt too big to fit in my skull, my head too heavy to rest on my shoulders. What? How? Oh God. O K, I'm coming home right now.

Needless to say, Ruth had done nothing to invite any of this. She was a fit, active person. I thought of her, once upon a time, as my Amazon; and though she was never exactly the sporty type, she enjoyed her ironical little boast that as a schoolgirl she had been junior high-jump champion of South Glamorgan. Like me, she used to cycle everywhere, and once or twice a week – before having children, at least – she might manage a swim. She ate well, didn't smoke, didn't drink much, and enjoyed sleep more than anyone I know. And there was no history of breast cancer in her family that we knew of.

To begin with, though, even Ruth having cancer did not cure us entirely of our optimism. It was rough – like doing twelve rounds with a heavyweight champ: every bit of bad news came like a body blow that would knock you down on the canvas, dazed and winded. But you would always pick yourself up before the count. Like suckers for the next punch, perhaps, but what else can you do?

First, it was secondary cancer, then Stage III. A few weeks

later, it was confirmed that she was Stage IV: the cancer had made the fatal leap from her left breast and its lymphatic system into another tissue type, the bone of her sternum. She already suspected it, from the characteristic pain of bone cancer that had already started. This set a pattern in which she always knew the bad news before the hospital tests confirmed it; her body told her – about the cancer in her lungs, her liver, and finally her brain.

By the end of July she was complaining regularly of headaches, and increasingly of insomnia too. But the former seemed to be controlled quite well by a low, 'maintenance' dose of steroids which reduced inflammation around the tumours, both in her brain and her liver. For a while it delayed the inevitable, giving Ruth another few weeks of her semblance of good health.

The unwritten rule of pharmacology, though, seems to be that you never get something for nothing. The price of taking steroids was first an unstoppable appetite – not Ruth's most notable area of self-control in any case – and ultimately a characteristic goitre of fat deposited around the jowls, the final indignity of losing her cheekbones altogether.

As for the sleep, more often than not, one of the children would still wake up in the night and need settling. With broken sleep being such an occupational hazard of parenthood, and the habit of sleeping soundly being so easy to lose and hard to relearn, I thought relatively little of it – except, of course, that it seemed not unnatural that Ruth might be finding sleep difficult because of anxiety about 'being terminal'. For a few days, at least, a doctor's prescription of Valium did seem to help with that.

But that week, in early August, I didn't know it but Ruth had been struggling to write her *Observer* column. The rough draft, unfinished, was to be her last. Writing was so swift and sure and natural to her, that it must have amplified her anxiety and her sense that something was truly awry that suddenly she couldn't stitch it together before lunch, as she had always been able to do.

I left for work on the Friday with no more sense of foreboding than the usual dull, grey, back-of-the-mind awareness of our predicament. Ruth generally looked after the children on Fridays, though increasingly with help from her mother. She would work the rest of the week, but taking a long weekend was the compromise she'd decided on between career and motherhood.

It was her mother who called me that afternoon to tell me that Ruth had checked herself into Guy's Hospital, where she had received all her treatment, because she was suffering from more and more frequent panic attacks. She'd even spoken of her fear of losing control and jumping out of the window. By the time I got there, the doctors had posted a registered mental nurse outside her door – an automatic measure when someone has expressed, even hypothetically, a suicidal urge.

I was shocked: how had this happened so suddenly? Why had I not seen it coming? I can't explain it, except perhaps that Ruth had been grimly hanging on as long as she could, struggling to keep a lid on the mental disintegration, until she lost her grip and, in an instant, confusion took over.

I don't remember much about that evening. Ruth must have been sedated – she was prescribed more Valium to help her sleep. My first thought, evidently that of the psychiatrist who had seen her too, was that sleep deprivation and generalised anxiety had precipitated a sort of nervous breakdown. It seemed so understandable. She'd toughed it out for so long, perhaps a collapse of some sort was inevitable.

And yet, that just didn't seem Ruth. Even in her most desperate moments, in the week after the twins were born, when again she'd hardly slept for days and felt herself to be going mad, she never seemed so to me. But this was different: as the weekend wore on, her nights were better and she slept a sedated sleep, but the Ruth we knew was replaced by this dull, flat, compliant person I didn't recognise at all.

By the Monday morning anxious conferences between

Ruth's sister Justine, her mother Hilary and I had led to the conviction that the brain tumour must be involved. At times I became haunted by something in Ruth's blank expression and uncomprehending, frightened eyes that I had seen somewhere before: they reminded me of nothing so much as some footage of a cow in the final stages of BSE, lurching and stumbling, knowing nothing but its incomprehension and fear. That sounds a terrible way to speak of someone you love, but there is nothing more terrible than to find that person spirited away and a brain-damaged, zombie-like *doppelgänger* usurping their place.

Ruth had cheerfully repeated in her column her oncologist's view that the liver tumours would probably get her before the brain ones. But now Ruth *was* going bonkers after all, and it wasn't to be the lurid paranoia of schizophrenia or the affective excess of mania; it was the blunted, stupid morbidity of the lobotomised. For that was what the tumour was doing to Ruth, stealthily performing its own crude version of a frontal lobotomy.

It meant she would never recover her ability to write, and – apart from a few two- or three-line e-mails during her last weeks in September – the last work that Ruth managed after she had checked herself into hospital was to write a handful of short letters to her children, Joe and Lola, to me, to her mother, her sister, her father, and two of her oldest friends Carrie and Jenny. Written in a slightly erratic hand, in short, chopped sentences and naive vocabulary, but full of the deepest love and generosity, they are desperate final messages from a woman who feels her mind drowning. That was her cancer's last cruel trick, gratuitously to add the insult of dementia to the injury of terminal illness.

Surgery, of course, was out of the question: even if neurosurgery might have been able to help someone with a brain tumour like Ruth's, the hard fact of her case was that, at best, her liver cancer would allow her only a couple of months more. In that context, a major operation was in nobody's interest. But radiotherapy was still an option. Of all the therapies to which Ruth had been subjected, it was the one type of treatment which, arguably, had been effective – the bone pain had been swiftly zapped and, over time, even the original breast tumour had shrivelled to insignificance.

While the liver cannot be irradiated without life-threatening consequences, brain tumours may respond well. There is some danger, we were told, that as the brain tissue is 'cooked' by the cobalt rays, it swells, and pressure inside the skull may build up to the extent that epilepsy and other symptoms of impaired brain function will occur. In the circumstances – that Ruth's brain function was already impaired and only likely to deteriorate further without treatment – it seemed vital to move as quickly as possible. One drawback of radiotherapy, however, is that its effect is cumulative and slow-acting: it might take two to three weeks at least before we would see any effect from treatment. But if there were still even a possibility, we felt, that radiotherapy might restore Ruth's reason, then it would be worth the gamble.

Once we'd determined on that course, our impatience to get started was acute. But when the radiologist ordered a CT scan as, we thought, a preliminary to treatment, it showed much less distortion and swelling in the brain than was expected given Ruth's disturbed state of mind. Progress was stalled for another day, and it was not until a psychiatric consultation confirmed that Ruth's symptoms – confused ideas, thought processes blocked in repetitive cycles, a strange lack of inhibition, a veering between childish dependency and a sullen aggressiveness – were classically consistent with frontal lobe damage, that radiotherapy was approved.

At times, our frustration and sense of thwarted urgency were almost unbearably intense, but perhaps it was right to proceed cautiously and by a kind of collective, consultative process. It seemed ironic to me, even then, that one of the most high-tech tests available, a CT scan, could have been so misleading – only for us to be put back on the right track by the much less precise, but ineffably more sensitive, diagnostic skills of a psychiatrist.

In the meantime, Ruth's condition fluctuated dramatically. First thing in the morning she would get the nurse to tell her what the day and date was. This she would write down on her hand, sometimes together with an instruction to herself like 'Matt's in charge' or 'Matt and Justine are in charge'. Whenever confusion overwhelmed her, which was all the time, she would return to this mantra. It seemed to calm her down for a few minutes, before she would set off again on the agitated, ultimately nonsensical round of questions-and-answers that troubled her.

At times, this placing of faith in me and her sister was sweet and touching, and in some small way made the fact that we were now taking all the important decisions for our indomitable Ruth a little easier to bear. But at other times, she would lapse into sullen hostility, a sign of the resentment she felt, but did not understand, that she had lost control of her life.

At the same time, Ruth became, in the technical parlance of psychiatry, 'disinhibited'. Her sense of what was socially appropriate behaviour lapsed. At times, this was trivial: one might notice, for instance, that she could be quite careless of whether she'd put on her knickers under her nightshirt when she sat on the bed to talk to a doctor. But on another occasion, she was cringe-makingly, comically rude to the Professor of Oncology.

The odd thing was that, even as her personality was disintegrating, this abrasiveness was so true to Ruth. She had always had, by her own proud admission, a 'problem with authority'. After that uncomfortable encounter, we had to try and coach her not to be hostile to doctors who, however legitimate Ruth's feelings of having been let down by the hospital in the past may have been, were clearly trying to do their best for her now.

Again, Ruth was constantly making lists while she was in hospital – lists of what she knew about her condition, lists of the drugs she had been prescribed, lists of priorities, even lists of guests for the children's second birthday party later in the month. That, too, was so Ruth. Except that now her lists were not the agenda-making of the aspirant superwoman, but a desperate effort to order her thoughts and maintain some purchase on reality.

But whatever she wrote on her hand, and whatever decisions were being taken about her treatment, the reality was that Ruth was still in charge. By Wednesday lunchtime she had decided that she was coming home, and – though we were waiting anxiously for the say-so of the psychiatrist – Ruth reached such a pitch of desperation that she marched off down the corridor towards the lifts. At that point she could not even be persuaded to travel in her sister's car: she was leaving now and she wanted to walk. After much agitation and a minor scuffle with the mental nurse, we were absolutely petrified that some doctor might wade in and demand that Ruth be restrained and, worst of all, confined to a psychiatric ward.

But in another minute she was mollified when I agreed to walk with her the mile or so from Guy's to our home in Walworth. I didn't know whether this was sensible, but it seemed the only way of avoiding an ugly and potentially disastrous scene there at the hospital.

It was a warm August day. We held hands and Ruth smiled all the way home, triumphant and happy as she could be. The RMN, an intelligent and humane young woman, followed at a discreet fifteen paces behind in case Ruth bolted. We must have made an odd little parade, and, for those who knew, a pathetic one, but like many terrible things, with hindsight, it has a tinge of comedy.

As far as Ruth was concerned, by then, it was the hospital that was making her anxious and confused. She was sure she would feel better in her own familiar environment. But home and hearth worked its soothing balm for only a few hours. It soon became obvious that her dissociated thoughts and agitation were not an unwanted side-effect of hospitalisation.

That she was still afflicted by the 'disinhibition' which the psychiatrist had noticed became graphically obvious when Ruth started eating the leftovers of the children's supper of baked beans and sausages. Ruth had been a vegetarian since her teens: a fortnight earlier and a mouthful of sausage would have made her gag. Now she was bolting them down with a steroid-fuelled compulsion.

Whereas before, in the hospital, Ruth had seemed always to rally for a visit by Joe and Lola and give at least an appearance of normality, it was now clear that they were in danger of seeing their mother distressed by her own inability to make sense. It was painfully obvious that we had to find another solution. Falling back on the safety net of the hospital's own palliative care outreach unit, we were told about Trinity Hospice in Clapham.

We went to see the hospice on Thursday. Ruth and I saw one of the doctors about her possible admission, and Ruth started to tell her about her illness and its progress. At first, Ruth was almost as fluent as she had ever been. Then, as she got more up-to-date, gradually she stumbled, until suddenly she could not frame in words a single other thought. It was like watching a truck running into sand. I hardly needed to complete the story for the doctor's benefit.

The decision to 'put' Ruth in the hospice was simply excruciating, even after a second near-sleepless night at home waiting for the tranquillisers to quell her ceaselessly reiterative babble. To place an elderly relative in an old people's home must approach that guilt and anguish, but at least that decision must feel as though it conforms in some way to 'the natural course of things'. To have to put your 33-year-old partner, your co-parent, your best friend, your peer and equal in every way, into care is pure distilled misery. Even when everyone agrees that you're doing the right thing, that this is the only sensible solution, it will still remain the loneliest decision in the world. By law, of course, no one can be confined in a hospice, but it felt as though I was locking up my wife like the mad woman in the attic.

And so, on Friday morning, following radiotherapy, I drove her over to Trinity Hospice, and left her to go and collect the children from nursery and put them to bed. It was exactly a week since Ruth had first checked herself into Guy's.

The next couple of days saw Ruth pull back from the brink of dementia. She became calm and gentle, sweet-natured even. It was not the raving Ruth we'd just endured, but neither was this spaced-out, tranquillised Ruth, emptied of all her fierce, headstrong will, her either. For a week now, we had been coming to terms with the possibility that the person we loved might be gone for good, her brain irreparably damaged by the intruding mass of tumorous cells. Though I often felt like crying, in the peaceful surroundings of the hospice's beautiful garden, I choked back my tears: I'd learnt that, in this state, they only confused and upset her as she tried to empathise without being able to understand the reason for my breaking heart. Her sister and her mother knew the same.

After a few days more, she gradually found some of that will again – enough at least to insist on reducing her drug intake and coming back home. And so, for a couple of weeks, we bounced backwards and forwards from home to hospice – under the endlessly kind, patient and compassionate guidance of the doctors and nurses there. For me, it was still a stressful and often miserable phase: I became, more than ever, the unpopular guardian, but I can see in retrospect that Ruth was gradually recovering her mind.

Yet it was a desperately haphazard process. At times, it seemed as though Ruth was back to her bolshy self. On one occasion, after I'd gone to work leaving my mother to supervise Ruth, with the children at the nursery, Ruth suddenly decided that she was going to go to the bank. Nothing my mother could say would dissuade Ruth and, although by then her tumour load meant that she was clearly in physical decline and beginning to struggle with climbing the stairs, off she marched, fired up with fury, to the Elephant & Castle shopping centre.

Instantly, my mum called me, and we agreed that she should simply follow Ruth at a discreet distance to make sure nothing awful happened. This she did, having to act like some low-budget parody of a private detective, following Ruth to the bank, watching while she paid in a couple of cheques, and then following her back out.

Then suddenly Ruth seemed to be at a loss, her sense of purpose evaporated. Seeing perhaps the buses on the other side of the road, she was just about to step recklessly into the road, when my mother ran up and caught her. My mum pretended to be there 'by coincidence', but it hardly mattered, because Ruth, suddenly weary, seemed to have forgotten all her earlier anger and was quite glad to see her. They walked slowly home together.

That was a typical episode: Ruth demanding her independence and deeply resenting any encroachment, even when thwarted not so much by us as by her own incapacity. She had to foster that conflict, I think, simply to stay alive. It was, in a way, motivational.

But there were brighter moments, especially in the last week or two when the radiotherapy seemed to have run its course and much of her essential self was restored. The first time we used her borrowed wheelchair, to take the children for a walk in St James's Park and to see the floral tributes to Princess Diana outside the gates of Buckingham Palace, she and her mother wept with laughter at the absurdity of the situation: Ruthie in a wheelchair!

The children, too, thought it a marvellous novelty to ride in 'Mummy's pushchair' and fought for turns. It was extraordinary to see them adapting so quickly to each new episode in the desperate narrative of Ruth's decline. They were only just two, yet for almost half their lives they'd lived with the fact that Mummy was sick. They had hardly known anything else, even though Ruth had carried on an astonishingly convincing impersonation of a fit, healthy person until her mental collapse. Only a couple of weeks earlier, she had been carrying Joe on her shoulders for miles along a beach on the Gower Peninsula in Wales where we were on holiday.

Often, though, Ruth treated us grown-ups more with impatience and irritation than anything else. The survivors have their guilt, the dying their justifiable anger. Since I now found myself making decisions for her, with only her grudging consent, I was often her 'gaoler'. I wrote a series of long, self-pitying e-mails to an overseas friend. She had the courage to tell me what I already knew, but could not quite bring myself to frame in words: that I had probably had as much love now from Ruth as I was going to have. Once again, the fantasy of terminal *tendresse* fell far short of the mark.

Hard as this was to accept then, I can find some pattern, some rationality, in it now. The dying person has to break her bonds with the world, to separate herself off: it is the process of alienation I still bitterly regret, but it is also a necessary part of letting go.

I was seeing this happening slowly in front of my eyes with the children. Day by day, as Ruth weakened physically under the load of her liver tumour, she could do less and less for the twins: no more bending to pick them up, no more rising at night to settle them, no more being the climbing frame and punchbag. Gradually, they too became accustomed to her being sick and unable to do all that mummy stuff.

On the night before the night she died, she struggled up the stairs in my parents' house, resting every other step, to help me put the children to bed. We were visiting there as a consolation for the fact that we'd finally cancelled a weekend in Ireland which Ruth had planned for months and held out in front of herself as another carrot of survival. I couldn't confront her with my misgivings about the Irish expedition: to cross her about anything felt like pulling the last cigarette from the condemned man's lips.

I lifted Joe to be cradled on her lap, and moved away to an adjacent bed to give Lola her customary half-pint of milk.

With the lights down, our bedtime ritual would always include singing the children's favourite nursery rhymes and lullabies. Ruth, who knew music, would lead and usually berate me at some point for my bum notes or tuneless dirging. Now I led, and she palely followed.

After a few minutes, Joe simply got up off Ruth's lap, came over and lay down on the bed by me and Lola. The sight of Ruth's poor, hunched silhouette, half-lit by a shaft of light from the door, still faintly finishing the lines of our song, was the saddest thing I ever hope to see. I knew then that, like Eurydice, she was lost to the Underworld, and that the true meaning of dying is its absolute loneliness.

As the children started their night's sleep, I looked for signs in Ruth of the bitter sorrow I felt. I found none; I think she had already made her peace with all that.

Ruth died just before 4 a.m. on 22 September, a Monday. Her mother was by her side. I had left earlier as she slipped into a morphine-rich sleep, never to wake again. Seeing that the end was near, Hilary called me at about 2 a.m. asking whether I wanted to go back to be there, but I decided that there was nothing more I could do for Ruth by being there and that I needed my strength for the next day with the children. And every day after that.

It seemed an obvious step, to take the children to see their mother one more time. Perhaps it wasn't quite the done thing, but since death is a fairly impossible concept for two-year-olds, I felt that they were only going to begin to grasp what had happened if they saw Ruth cold and inanimate. Children, Ruth was fond of saying, are concrete little thinkers and don't need euphemisms. Circumlocution is for grown-ups; children just need the truth.

While it may help them now to understand that, for instance, their mother has not simply abandoned them wilfully, the truth, in any case, is that Joe and Lola are almost certainly too young to retain any direct memory of the room in the hospice where Hilary and the hospice nurses had laid Ruth out. By the time we arrived, past 9 a.m. with the rush-hour traffic, Ruth had been lying in cold repose for several hours. With her hamsterish cheeks, her scruffily cropped hair, and her lips palely parted, she looked suddenly very young, quite childlike. Not lovely, perhaps, as once she had been, but very peaceful.

Death is a hard concept for adults to grasp too. Through tear-blurred vision, it was easy to imagine that she might suddenly sit up and order a glass of fruit juice or a mug of hot chocolate. It takes not minutes, nor even months, but perhaps years for one to register and accept, at every stratum and substratum of one's being, the loss of a loved one. Even now it feels unreal most of the time. How could it have happened, after all? It wasn't part of the plan.

Like Ruth, I have no religion, but I can more easily understand than ever the appeal of the idea of an afterlife. Not that it doesn't still seem a magnificent fiction, but without it it is so hard to imagine where all that dynamism, all that spirit, energy and force of personality that was Ruth could have gone. Can it be that it simply leaches away entropically?

In truth – and she knew it – Ruth's afterlife is in her children. It was a bitter-sweet comfort, for they are the thing she could least bear to give up. Her family she'd had for thirty-three years; me she'd had for twelve. But her darling twins she'd known for barely two years – a speck in time. In a curious way, though, because they are twins, non-identical twins, one can see how much of Joe and Lola is simply a fact of genetic inheritance: they share the same environment and a perfectly parallel history, and yet they are already such fascinatingly divergent, individualised little people.

Whatever Ruth could have given by way of nurture, they were already richly endowed by her gift of nature. That they will always be her children is her piece of the future, and our piece of her.